THE CHURCH FINANCE IDEA BOOK

Wayne C. Barrett

DISCIPLESHIP RESOURCES
MATERIALS FOR GROWTH IN CHRISTIAN FAITH & LIFE
—— NASHVILLE, TENNESSEE ——
P.O. BOX 840 • NASHVILLE, TN 37202 • PHONE (615) 340-7068

Also available from Discipleship Resources:

Celebrate Giving, by Herb Mather and Don Joiner.
A complete financial commitment campaign.

Celebrate Together, by Herb Mather and Don Joiner.
A financial campaign using group settings.

Celebrate and Visit, by Juanita Ivie and Don Joiner.
An every member visitation program.

Christians and Money, by Don Joiner.
A guide to personal finance.

More Money, New Money, Big Money, by Wayne C. Barrett.
Creative strategies for funding today's church.

Reprinted 1995.

ISBN 0-88177-065-5

Library of Congress Catalog Card No. 88-72382

DR065

CONTENTS

PART SIX: PLANNED GIVING STRATEGIES
FOR TODAY AND TOMORROW

APPENDICES

INTRODUCTION

In recent years, local church finance has moved in several directions. Financial campaigns are often tolerated. The Finance Committee, or other task group of the church in charge of "raising the budget," waits until the last minute, rushes through a quick program, and hopes the finances will somehow equal expenses by the end of the year. Another response is to limit local church financing and fund-raising to a specialized area of church life. The church either "hires" a professional or avoids doing anything until the church is in a financial crisis.

Some churches have been seeking the "mythical" solution to their funding concerns. This type of church thinks it can avoid any dealing with financial concerns and seeks to deal only with spiritual and "stewardship" issues. They too avoid any action until there is a financial crisis.

For many years local church fund-raising was limited to the Every Member Visitation (EMV). This has been the most successful fund-raising approach for most churches. Then along came a variety of "circuit" type programs. Packets are passed from house to house. Members hope that other members will not be home, so they can stick the packet in the storm door or mailbox and run. Many churches used this approach long past its effectiveness. If your congregation has used one or both of these approaches past their effectiveness, there are other options!

Lyle Schaller has recently shown how future trends in funding for the church will include, but not exclusively use, the annual financial campaign for raising the necessary funds to keep the local church in ministry. If the annual fund-raising campaign is not your only way to raise funds, what are the other alternatives?

Wayne Barrett has captured a wide variety of possibilities in this "encyclopedia" of funding. Wayne has many years of experience in the church's life. I trust his intuitive knowledge of the financial life of a local church. He has been an active layman, ordained pastor, administrator, and fund-raiser in churches of all sizes. He is considered an expert in the field of local church fund-raising. He brings to this book a wealth of ideas, yet places these ideas in words and descriptions which any member of your finance committee could understand. There is a good mix, as he keeps a perspective on stewardship and yet maintains the overall goal of raising funds for the church's ministry.

From cultivation to communication, from fund-raising to fund-management, from budgeting to spending, this book has what your church needs to effectively fund your church's ministry.

Donald W. Joiner
Nashville, TN

PART ONE

Commitment Campaign Strategies

1. EVERY MEMBER COMMITMENT—THE WINNER AND STILL CHAMPION

Year after year this hoary old device continues to raise more money than any other method. What is its genius? While one suspects that many dynamics combine to make the EMC a success, the principal strengths of the program are:

1. Everyone is involved. The sheer numbers of including all persons generates tremendous potential. Many persons are making the campaign work. Folks get involved as callers, leaders, hosts/hostesses, child care workers—they are involved by doing.

2. The plan forces the church to be intentional about the future. Tasks such as budgeting, planning, and program interpretation cannot be avoided.

3. There is interpretation of what the church's ministry is trying to accomplish. It is amazing how little regular interpretation of the ministry occurs throughout the year. The EMC often is the only vehicle which presents the ministry to the people in a manner that they can understand.

4. There is opportunity for feedback. Because even inactive members are a part of the campaign, they have a medium through which they may communicate with church leaders. Although we may not like what we hear from these "inactives," we need to hear because they too are the grassroots.

An overview of a successful Every Member Commitment campaign follows. Because an abundance of excellent literature is available describing the EMC, only a brief description will be included here.

ORGANIZATION

No matter how strong the temptation may be to begin work immediately, no planning should be done until you are certain that you know what you are trying to accomplish. It may seem completely obvious that your goal is to secure pledges of financial support for the congregation's ministry. However, you really have two purposes: 1) to secure the pledges, *and* 2) to interpret the ministry of the congregation in such a way as to make the people want to pledge. Any campaign which attempts to do one of these functions without the other is missing the point.

If there is any doubt concerning the necessity of interpretation as well as securing pledges, consider the reality that a pledge, by itself, will produce no money at all. The pledger must sustain the pledge by *paying* it, or the pledge is worthless. Where proper interpretation precedes the pledge, a higher percentage gets paid.

Just as a campaign may fail from doing too little, campaigns fail also from doing too much. A campaign which attempts to secure support for the general fund, building fund, a mission emphasis, and some other capital item is sending out too many signals. The donor cannot comprehend all that is being interpreted. Keep your message as simple and carefully focused as possible.

RECRUITMENT

If you know what you are trying to do, the next step is to recruit the best possible team of persons to help do it. As described elsewhere, a campaign run entirely by the finance committee, for the finance committee, will seldom succeed.

It is absolutely vital that the EMC leadership be representative of the whole congregation. This is necessary for the following reasons:

1. The EMC is a total-church event. It needs (and deserves) the best efforts of everyone.

2. The funds secured through the EMC will underwrite the programs of the non-financial leaders. They have a stake in making the EMC a success.

3. If the leadership has not participated in securing the support for their programs, a dangerous adversary relationship can develop between the program leadership and the finance committee.

4. When the campaign clearly is representative of the entire congregation, the donors recognize that their pledge supports their church, not just the finance committee.

Recognize that a comprehensive EMC will require many different skills. At the very minimum you will need persons with:

- Verbal skills—both oral and written
- Organizational skills—people who can see the "Big Picture"
- Detail and follow-through skills—many campaigns fail here
- Motivational skills—the troops need inspiration

Additional skills, while not absolutely necessary, often include:

- Child care
- Refreshment preparation and service
- Clerical/telephone
- Computer programming and data processing

No individuals will possess all or even a majority of these skills. It is ideal to recruit leaders with the expectation that they will possess only *one* of these skills, but that skill in abundance. In fact, it is a dangerous temptation to allow any one member of the team to be responsible for more than one key component. The loss of such an individual (or more likely, the overloading) could spell disaster. Resist the temptation to allow a willing and multi-talented person to be responsible for too many components of the program.

The following chart illustrates the organization required for an effective EMC and the positions involved.

TRAINING AND MOTIVATION

All members of the team, from general chairperson to visitor to refreshment hostess, have a need (and a right) to receive training which will enable them to perform their task effectively. In some cases this will only require a clear description of the task. In other situations only a "pep talk" for motivation will be necessary. Most persons, however, will require a clear job description, training sufficient to accomplish the task, and motivation to encourage the performance in an enthusiastic manner.

Unless you have an unusually small team, it is prudent to schedule duplicate training sessions at differing times. This allows for the inevitable schedule conflicts and enables all team members to receive training.

 You will have much better results in recruiting if you can promise (and deliver!) adequate training. No one wants to go into battle unarmed.

ORGANIZATIONAL CHART

EXECUTIVE COMMITTEE:
  Pastor(s)
  6 Chairpersons
  5 Division Leaders

PERSONNEL:
  5 Division Leaders
  25 Captains (couples)
  100 Visitors (couples)

Executive Committee
General Chairpersons

Child Care Coord.		Proposal Chr.
Arrangements Chr.		Prayer Chr.
Youth Coord.		Advance Chr.

Visitation Chr.

Division Leader	Division Leader	Advance Division

Division Leader	Division Leader	Division Leader

NOTE: This organization is for a large church. You may need to scale down the number of divisions and visitors proportionately.

"Mind saving this till AFTER our financial drive?"

PROMOTION

One of the most important lessons I learned from a student charge was that everybody is not "just like me." Pastors would do well to remember that while they may be "print-oriented," not everyone gets information by reading. What this suggests is that something more than the church newsletter will be required for adequate promotion of your EMC.

Try to use every medium you can think of: newsletters, direct mail, "minute man" announcements during worship, posters, displays, interpretive programs, announcement or question-answer sessions at other church meetings, discussion during church school classes.

Recognize that your product is not the *budget* but the ministry. You are not promoting numbers but *persons* whose lives will be enriched by the ministry of your church, made possible by the stewardship of your fellow parishioners.

THE INTENSIVE PHASE—VISITATION AND REPORTING

You have planned, you have organized, you have secured the leadership of the "best people," you have trained and motivated the leadership, and you have also promoted the campaign in every way imaginable. Now you are ready for what you *thought* you were attempting in the first place.

Each family (singles, couples, extended families living together) will be visited during this crucial Intensive Phase. Divide your total prospect list so that no caller must visit more than half a dozen prospects. To ask any more will be counter-productive.

Before your visitors make their calls, however, they have a right to expect that the following has occurred:

1. Every member and prospect has been alerted that the campaign is coming. At least a mailing has already announced this campaign.

2. A pledge card has been received by every prospect. (The visitors will still need to bring one along.)

3. At least some materials have been provided for visitors to use in interpreting the program of the church. (Note: Just in case questions arise—the program is not the primary purpose of the visits.)

You should take special care to ensure that your visitors know what is expected. The call will be a success if real communication occurs. Callers should be reassured that they need not "bring back a scalp" to have succeeded. In fact, they must be warned against high-pressuring prospects in such a way that a pledge is received but only at the cost of hard feelings.

Schedule a week for all visits to take place. This brief time will give ample flexibility to allow for persons not home or hard to reach, yet still give the clear signal that all calls are to be completed by a reasonable date. Schedule times for callers to report back the results of their visits. Ideally the church will be open every evening of the week to allow for reporting, extra training, and perhaps a "pep talk."

Recognize that at least part of the purpose of the reporting sessions is to accomplish far more than reporting. Callers need support and encouragement. It's much easier to do it at a central location than to chase them all over town to do it. The sessions also provide an opportunity to check to see if the calls are being made. Don't underestimate the reluctance many visitors may feel about calling on "strangers." Monitor carefully to make certain that calls are getting made. If a caller fails to appear at a reporting session by the middle of the week, a phone call is in order to inquire if the visits are being made.

VICTORY SUNDAY

For years the conventional wisdom was that pledges must come back via the visitation process. In some situations with shut-ins, schedule difficulties, etc., this may still be the easiest procedure. But because we want donors to *bring* not send in their pledges, you need to designate a Sunday on which persons may bring their pledges to church.

Remember that we have not encouraged our callers to insist upon a pledge but rather to remind the donor that everyone will be *bringing* the pledges to worship the next Sunday. A weakness of this system is the potential that a poorly motivated donor will make no pledge at all. Yet let us recall that the goal is not merely to get the donor to pledge but to *pay* the pledged amount. (Check the Income Increase Matrix.) Thus the seeming dilemma of the unreturned pledge is mitigated by the fact that poorly motivated pledgers are typically poorly motivated givers as well and seldom pay a high percentage of a non-representative pledge.

Victory Sunday will result in receipt of 75-90% of pledges all at once. This is a marvelously efficient way to receive pledges but also allows for immediate announcement of totals. Receive the pledges early in the service and have a team of counters tabulate the pledge totals. Announce the amount pledged at the end of the service. If possible, indicate how that total compares with last year's pledges from the same persons.

FOLLOW-UP

Victory Sunday will tell you how much work lies ahead for you. Every prospect who has not returned a pledge by now, either in person on Victory Sunday or through the visitor the previous week, must be contacted once again.

It is important that *the same visitor contact* these persons. At this point we increase the pressure somewhat. The caller makes it clear that we want a pledge card returned. The response on that card is not the issue now.

Remember we have already received 75-90% of our pledges, but we want this person's response.

The caller may find the telephone will assist in this process of follow-up. A phone call tells the prospect three important facts:

1. We recognize the pledge has not yet been returned.
2. We want the pledge irrespective of the response.
3. We are prepared to come and pick it up.

Allow the prospect the option of bringing the pledge to worship the next Sunday, but make it clear that you will come by for it if it is not delivered. This is not intended to be a threat but rather to convey to the prospect your conviction that this pledge is important business vital to the church's future planning.

The next Sunday, you will receive nearly all the pledges you are going to get. A few will still need to be picked up, but most pledge cards received through visitors at this stage either will be returned blank or with a token pledge not likely to be paid. Note: It is still worth the effort to pick these up for at least three reasons:

1. We need to confirm our contention that pledges are important. If they are important, this is in spite of the amount pledged.

2. We have tried to communicate to the prospect that our concern is for *them*, not merely their pledge. To abandon them now will undermine everything we have accomplished.

3. We must complete our end of the covenant. We have said, "Return the pledge card." Even a blank, signed card that is returned has completed the prospect's covenant. We must complete ours by making the effort to receive it.

WRAP-UP

By now you know what you've got. It is to be hoped that the pledge totals at least equal your goals. I have enjoyed the experience of over-subscribing the projected budget, and my prayer is that you will know such a mountaintop experience.

Report back to your donors at least four messages:

1. How much was pledged by the congregation (the dollar amount).
2. What these funds will enable (the ministry planned).

3. How much your records show the individual prospect pledged. It is vital that you report this to ensure no misunderstanding.

4. A sincere statement of appreciation for the prospect/donor's participation in the campaign. To fail to say "thank you" will be to fail in the entire campaign—it is that important.

You are now ready to begin the task of administering the finances of the congregation for the rest of the year. By the way, it's really not too early to *begin planning next year's campaign.* Good luck.

2. NEMV—*NOT* EVERY MEMBER VISITATION

When someone asks my wife, How's your husband? her most typical response is, "Better than nothing." It has been my observation that visitation of any kind in a congregational stewardship development program is better than no visitation at all. However, before you presume that the only alternative to an every member visitation program is no visitation program at all, I suggest another alternative. The *Not* Every Member Visitation Plan is not as good as an Every Member Visitation Plan, but it recognizes the unique differences in need of different groups within a congregation. It also recognizes the built-in limitations in human resources that local finance leadership may face.

The *Not* Every Member Visitation Plan recognizes that there are probably no fewer than five different groups within your congregation, each with a particular pattern of behavior, style of interest, and opportunity for communication. This plan assumes that to call on *some* of these persons with a message more closely tailored to their unique situation would be more productive than to call on everyone with a standardized message. It also recognizes, without being cynical, that in many cases the alternative to calling upon everyone is not to call at all.

Below we have demonstrated for you a graphic representation of the five groups within your congregation. Each of them approximates about ⅕ of your membership.

OLD FAITHFULS

The first group, you will carefully note, is a group made up of the top 20% of your givers, the group we will' call "Old Faithfuls." Old Faithfuls are not necessarily old, but they are always faithful. And while they represent the top 20% of our givers financially, they are not necessarily those who give the highest percentages of their income. They are the easiest ones to identify because we simply count down the top 20% of our givers and that becomes the group we identify as Old Faithfuls. It is not unusual in a congregation for this 20% of the membership to account for 70% and even 80% of your congregation's income.

The Five Segments of Your Congregation

Old Faithfuls	Great Lakes	Kansas	Sleeping Bear	Death Valley
70 + % of Congregation's Income	10-20% of Congregation's Income	5-10% of Congregation's Income	5% or less of Congregation's Income	0% of Congregation's Income
1. Don't need a call	1. Call	1. Call	1. Call	1. Don't call
2. Ask their dreams	2. Encourage pledging; designated 2nd mile giving	2. Inform about programs	2. Stress "We care about you"	2. Refer to Evangelism Committee

The good news about Old Faithfuls is that they will continue to be faithful, they will continue to give, almost in spite of what we do. A visitation program that assumes we must solicit them and ask for a pledge misses the point. Their faithfulness suggests that they will continue to give, will continue to pledge, and will continue to discharge their stewardship responsibilities because they want to, because they're used to doing so, and because they intend to, not because of our solicitation. I am convinced that the apparent success of many poorly thought-out campaigns is based primarily upon the fidelity of this most faithful group within a congregation. Their faithful giving tends to mask a lot of mistakes that we make in developing the remainder of the congregation. Yet the fact remains that this group does not need to be asked or begged to give. They will give almost in spite of us. In fact, if a church has a particular financial need, it is likely that the most efficient group to deal with in terms of an immediate and significant response will be this old faithful category of donors. Yet in congregation after congregation, the development pattern is just the opposite. We ask for our pledges and those who are most highly motivated will give them to us in any form we ask, typically in a worship service. Then we gear up to go out after those that did not come in, and in fact spend most of our efforts on the least productive fields of opportunity.

I have learned over time that the best thing to do with Old Faithfuls is to let them be faithful and to treat them with a degree of respect that they have earned. When you call upon Old Faithfuls, and I hope that you will, the proper context for your call is not to ask them for more money, but rather to ask their insight, opinion, and evaluation of the current directions and dreams for your church. You might very well begin the interview by asking, "What are your hopes, your dreams, your visions for our church?" Listen very carefully when they begin to respond to that question. They have earned the right to share, and they have also earned the right to be taken seriously. Coming out of this discussion, however, is our opportunity to challenge them, and I have found that one of the most effective ways to do that is to follow their statement of hope, dream, and vision with a question: "And what are you personally willing to give or do to make this happen?" This allows them to give direction to the leadership of the church but also properly puts the challenge upon those who have the dream and the hope. You will find that they often respond far beyond your dreams.

DEATH VALLEY

At the other end of this scale of five different groups is the opposite fifth of your congregation. If the top giving group can be characterized as Old Faithfuls, we could use this same analogy and identify the bottom giving group as Death Valley. This stratum of your congregation could be identified by these characteristics: They not only seldom attend but typically never attend or at least have not attended with any record of it in the last twelve months. They do not give and have not supported the church with financial contributions of record in the last twelve months. Often these persons are younger than the average for your membership, but that is not always the case. In many situations you will find they no longer even live in your community and it will be almost impossible for you to make contact with a home visit to them. This is no tremendous disadvantage because you should not call on these people at all in the context of your stewardship development program. Save the visit with these persons for a later, less controversial time in the life of your church. Perhaps call on them during January when you invite them to a special series of Lenten services. Or perhaps call on them some other time during the year when you have a message less challenging in terms of the financial commitment that you're seeking from the membership of your church.

The top stratum and the bottom stratum of your congregation are potential groups to take out of the visitation phase of your financial campaign. The Old Faithfuls don't need it and the Death Valley group won't benefit much from it. The most efficient grounds for visitation as a means for influencing increased giving will be the three remaining groups, each representing an additional 20% of your membership.

SLEEPING BEAR

Next to the Death Valley group is another underperforming stratum, the second poorest 20% of your givers. These folks we'll characterize with the name, Sleeping Bear Donors. They're sleeping; they're not dead yet; but there's no great vitality among these persons either. They tend to be younger than the average. They attend once a month or less. They almost always give when they attend, but they never give when they don't attend. These are persons who are ambivalent about the church. They're not against you; they may not even be against pledging; but they have no great enthusiasm for the ministry of the church or their part in discharging it.

This group is an ideal candidate for a home visit for a number of reasons. First, they need to know about the ministry of our church because it's *their* church as well. They have simply lost touch. By attending once a month or less, it's hard to keep up to date on what the various opportunities for ministry are within a person's congregation. Similarly, because they are younger than average, they often have children at home who need but frequently do not experience the educational ministries of the congregation. The goal, then, of your visit is not to solicit, not to inform about stewardship or heavy theological issues, but rather to reinforce the very simple fact that our church cares about its members, i.e., we care about you.

There are two more groups left, each approximating 20% of your membership. These groups are much less homogeneous in behavior than the previously mentioned groups. Because of wide variety of behavior, it is difficult to establish a single message appropriate for all who fall into these categories, yet experience has shown that there is a strategy that can be successful for each segment.

GREAT LAKES

The second highest giving group we'll call the Great Lakes donors because of their tremendous, though currently unrealized, potential. When you chart the giving pattern of your congregation by category, you will note a dramatic drop-off in the giving of this group compared with the Old Faithfuls directly above them. "Great Lakes" members attend regularly (though not every week), are often willing to pledge (but the amount is not great), and frequently assume leadership positions in the congregation.

There are two strategies that are appropriate for "Great Lakes" donors. First, encourage pledging. These persons make the greatest growth in giving when they build giving into their intentional "spending plan." Until they are willing to make a giving commitment, there is little hope for major increases in their giving level.

Next, challenge these donors with Designated Giving opportunities. Because of their regular attendance pattern and relatively low levels of pledged giving, this group has high potential for second-mile giving. The operative fund-raising concept for Great Lakes donors is "up-grade"—to attempt to get these donors to increase the level of their current giving.

KANSAS

The final stratum of members in your church is right in the middle of your congregation, so we'll call them "Kansas" donors. While a wide-ranging category, they tend to resemble the following profile: They attend once or twice per month, give whenever they attend (though seldom when they don't attend), frequently are found in the $3-5 per week level of givers.

For "Kansas" donors recognize that these persons are primarily "consumers." They are willing to pay for what they receive from the church, but seldom fully appreciate what is available for them. Here you might concentrate on interpreting the program of your church in an attempt to increase the "Kansas" members' level of participation (see Barrett's Law, p. 57). The payoff can be great, with increases in giving of up to 100% as participation increases.

Another strategy appropriate for "Kansas" donors is Monthly Statements. It will not be part of the NEMV but rather supports your efforts with regular statements (and return envelopes) throughout the year. This strategy is particularly important if "Kansas" donors are age 50 or less.

For five donor segments, use five visitation strategies for your implementation. Be sure to remember that the point of the *Not* Every Member Visitation is the awareness that, in most congregations, there is no one stewardship message for all. Experience shows that fewer calls made in which the right message is delivered will result in better results than in a campaign in which a unified message is shared. Recognize that your congregation is heterogeneous and act accordingly. You'll notice the difference right away.

3. THE "SADDLEBAG" METHOD

This popular means of receiving financial commitments is known by a variety of names—Pony Express, Circuit Rider, Iron Horse, Run for the Roses, and many more. The basic elements of those campaigns, however, are essentially the same. The congregation is divided into several chains or groupings of households. The first family on this list completes their commitment card and then delivers the packet of campaign materials to the next family on the list, which does the same for family number three, and so on.

The sheer simplicity of this strategy makes it an excellent way for a congregation to begin the process of emphasizing every member commitment without a formal visitation on each family. When properly organized, the entire campaign can be completed in a couple of weeks, with the commitment collection done in as little as one day. Because the only contact members have with other members is to receive or deliver the materials, there is little reason for confrontation or unpleasant experiences. Even the least committed members will be contacted and may participate.

It should be recognized, however, that this format is primarily a pledge *collection* system rather than an effort to interpret or encourage commitment. If you have a message to deliver, it is risky to expect the Pony Express or its clones to deliver it. Communication opportunities are limited to direct mail and are consequently "spotty" in getting the message delivered.

In addition, it is not unusual for the delivery system to break down. Like a chain, it is no stronger than its weakest link. It may be a bit much to expect an uncommitted member to take the time to deliver the campaign packet to the next house. Nevertheless, with trained "trail bosses" prepared to move the packets when a snag is encountered, the circuit can be completed with relative ease.

We recommend the "Saddlebag Method" for congregations as a change of pace from those intensive campaigns, or as a first experience with every member contact. A variety of materials is available to help you organize your campaign.

4. GET THE "BEST PEOPLE"

Finance leaders are wonderful people. Yet few successful stewardship campaigns can afford the luxury of a drive staffed only with finance committee members.

"I THINK I'VE FOUND THE GUY TO LEAD OUR FUND-RAISING DRIVE."

Any careful examination of successful stewardship campaigns shows that success is a product of the efforts of many people. There is need for planners, for detail people, for behind-the-scenes and up-in-front types. Not a few crusades have gone down to defeat for lack of a spokesperson or an organizer or some other crucial skill not represented on the finance committee.

When planning your campaign, resolve to recruit only the "best" leadership. Willing but unqualified leadership is doomed. Give your key leaders responsibility for a *limited* number of tasks, adequate lead time, proper training and assistance, and the very best persons will say "yes."

Here is a partial list of the types of persons you should recruit.

1) A meeting chairperson whose primary job is to preside and make certain that other tasks are delegated.

2) A "spokesperson" to be the link between the committee and the congregation (should not be the Finance Chairperson).

3) A communications coordinator, for producing printed communications—brochures, letters, articles in the newsletter and bulletin.

4) A "credibility" specialist who is the most respected member of the congregation, perhaps the "grand old man" or "grand old woman" of the church, whose opinion is always respected.

5) Someone from the program arm of the congregation, perhaps the chair of the Council on Ministries.

6) Additional positions to represent the major areas within the congregation, where significant other expenditures are anticipated—personnel, trustees, etc.

5. GET GROUPS INVOLVED

Seventy-five years ago local churches were often financed (and dominated) by a small group of persons called the "Stewards." It was an honor to be invited to join the stewards but a financial sacrifice, too, because the stewards literally paid for the church.

This tradition is long past in most congregations, except for an unfortunate administrative relic. While not expected to give all the money personally, the finance committee in many churches is still solely responsible for raising the congregation's revenues. This is most unfortunate and wrong.

The worship committee is not expected to do all the worshiping for the congregation. The choir is expected to *lead,* not do all the singing. Similarly the finance committee has a perfect right to invite all groups within the church to find a way to express their corporate, as well as personal, stewardship.

Perhaps the choir could offer a benefit concert for a special project. Maybe the women's group could put on a fund-raising dinner. The youth might have a car wash or contribute free child care. The point is, the church needs the efforts of everybody to secure adequate financial resources.

When it's stewardship campaign time, each group in the church should be involved. Some churches cease all scheduled activity during a fund drive. In fact, I think just the opposite is most appropriate. Groups in the congregation should participate and *lead* throughout a crusade.

6. TEAM WORK

"Tinkers to Evers to Chance." Few phrases in sport possess that lyrical lilt or convey such an awesome truth as this well-worn scrap of lore. The irony is that Joe Tinker, John Evers, and Frank Chance were never in reality a particularly productive double-play team in baseball.

For the double-play to be achieved, each player within the trio must perform a particular task. The shortstop fields the grounder and flips to the second baseman for the force out. The second sacker relays the throw to the first baseman, whose catch completes the double-play. Note that an out can be secured at either base, but the double-play requires both bases to be touched.

No one knows how many congregations short-circuit the teamwork concept and content themselves with half the job. Typically the stewardship campaign is in the fall and, when the pledges are in, the work comes to a halt. How much better if the relay is made by turning names of those who failed to participate in the stewardship campaign to the evangelism committee. These persons ought to be visited during the year, with no financial context associated with the call. The message of the non-financial call ought to be something along the line of "We care about you." Paradoxically, this message is delivered best with a question, not a statement. "How are you?" can deliver much meaning when asked sincerely rather than as a pleasantry.

January and early February are excellent months to make this type of visit. Since the annual financial campaign is well behind you, it will be obvious that this call is not about money. In addition, the season of Lent is nearing, so you will have something inviting for less active members to share. Perhaps your visitors will want to bring special Lenten brochures or devotional literature. One church had excellent results by using a survey as the content of this visit.

Teamwork suggests that the finance committee and the evangelism committee might undertake this task together. One church forged a coalition of finance and evangelism members who agreed to make home visits twice a year. In the fall they called on behalf of the stewardship campaign, in the spring for evangelistic concerns. Each group developed a better appreciation for the interrelatedness of the two disciplines—and the church grew in attendance and income at a 15% annual rate!

7. THE $10,000 SECRET

The speaker was well-known as an expert in church fund-raising. His pitch? For only $10,000 he would direct our church finance campaign in such a way that we would greatly increase our income. His secret? "We use a method which results in greatly increased giving by 'token' donors—those who currently give one or two dollars per week," he said.

What was this $10,000 "secret"? It turned out to be something so simple we should have anticipated it, but it also turned out to be so successful it nearly paid for itself. The "secret" was the use of *giving units*.

Token givers tend to give the smallest amount they think they can get away with. The basic unit of token giving is currently the one dollar bill. (If you don't believe it, watch what you get for any spontaneous offering for which the givers have little enthusiasm.)

The genius of *giving units* is to redefine the basic units. For instance, what would happen if you asked your membership to pledge "units per week" rather than dollars? The token givers would still pledge only one unit. But what if the unit was $5? One unit suddenly becomes worth five times what it was before. The amazing thing is that token givers can usually pay five just as easily as one; the trick is to get them started.

Give your donors the option of a dollar amount but stress pledging in multiples of "units per week." You'll find that the person who really insists on giving $8.00 weekly will do so, but many pledges which otherwise would have been for $8.00 or $9.00 become two units—$10.00.

The best part of this technique is that it places the burden for increase upon those who most deserve it. Those who have given only token amounts now begin to assume a more realistic share of their financial responsibility.

8. PLEDGE INCREASE ONLY

One strategy that has success built right in is to ask your donors to pledge the dollar amount of their increase only. Thus a pledge of $15 per week compared to last year's $12 per week would be expressed for a $3 per week increase.

Why ask for an indication of increase only? The reasons are many and basic:

1. It presumes an increase. During inflationary times, a pledge of "the same as last year" is really a reduction.

2. It focuses on the amount increased and is not overwhelmed by the renewal portion of the pledge. An additional $3 per week may look a lot more manageable than the entire $15 per week.

3. It allows the increased amount to compete fairly with the rest of the donor's budget decisions. The appliance store is describing the increase only when it trumpets an item for "only $10 per week." Compared to the option of no purchase at all, this is an *additional* $10 per week. The church that asks for the pledge-as-increase helps the donor see all expenditures in the same light.

4. This technique tends to generate more increase from low level or token donors. While token givers tend to renew rather than increase their pledges, this technique often generates increases more commensurate with their abilities to give.

9. VISITATION—PRIMING THE PUMP

G.K. Chesterton once observed that Christianity has never been tried and found wanting. It's been found difficult and not tried. Many people have discovered that their church's visitation program is in much the same predicament. No one seriously argues that visitation is ineffective. Churches abandon it, however, because it is discovered to be a lot of work. But when work gives clear results, it's worth doing, and visitation is that kind of work.

However, what needs to be done to implement a visitation program in the local church? Assuming that we agree upon the value of it, first, recruit persons actually to implement the visitation. Here, too, our experience often gets in the way rather than assists us. Many persons in the church have had some experience making visitation or stewardship visits. Most of their experience, however, has not been good experience, and we'll need to help them overcome that context.

A church that has had absolutely miserable results in recruiting visitors might try to have their initial experience with visitation be separate from the church financial campaign or stewardship drive. In fact the best time might be late January or early February: the time of the year that is clearly identified as separate from the fall stewardship solicitation but is also a time when you have something worthwhile to promote, namely Lent. Under the context of calling attention to the special Lenten emphases and programs, you may call on everyone in the congregation without threatening them or without having the problem of "nothing to say."

A hundred years ago Methodist churches were led by a remarkable group of saints called the Stewards. There were typically eight in every church, and they had an awesome responsibility. To them was given the responsibility for generating all of the church's income. Each of those eight stewards was personally responsible for 12½% of the church's income that year. If money was not raised from the rest of the membership, those eight men, and they were nearly always men, had to make up the difference out of their own personal financial resources. Their strategy, however, was an extraordinary one. They took that same 12½% of the church's membership and visited them four times annually. During the first three of those visits, the stewards typically would inquire about the spiritual vitality of the family. What sort of devotional literature were they reading, what type of prayer life did they have, and so on. On the fourth visit, however, the steward inquired about the level of financial support that the family anticipated committing for the coming year. Inspired by the directness of that fourth visit and its financial consequences, few people objected to that type of question because the steward had clearly demonstrated his pastoral concern and care for the family in the three previous visits.

Today, however, we believe that we can get right down to the heart of the matter and we've often abandoned those first three visits. We instead call once a year, if that, and ask pointedly about financial support with little concern for welfare or spiritual vitality in the family. Is it any wonder that people often call us to task about this particular concept when they complain "you only come to see me when you want my money"?

Visitation ought to be a year-long process. It ought not to be owned by or performed by the finance committee by themselves. It is, instead, a part of the nurture and outreach of the congregation's entire ministry and legitimately should be shared by the entire leadership of the church. One church teamed up the stewardship finance committee with the evangelism committee, each covenanting to work together with the other during their particular time of the year of responsibility. The evangelism people worked with the finance committee during the fall's every member visitation, and the finance committee continued to work with the evangelism people during an ongoing visitation thrust throughout the year. This church achieved no less than a 26% increase in their giving the very first year and a corresponding 15% increase over and above that the second year.

10. WHAT TO SAY ON A STEWARDSHIP VISIT

Perhaps the biggest single reason for refusing to make stewardship home solicitations is the excuse, "I never know what to say." It is sad that we have led our callers to believe that they are to function as the ecclesiastical equivalent of door-to-door salespersons.

This anxiety can be managed if we are clear about our objective when we call. Our purposes are really two-fold: to secure a pledge and to communicate with our donors. But what are we to communicate?

Frequently callers are instructed to interpret the program of the church, to emphasize new ministries, and to "sell" the budget. There are, of course, some donors who appreciate and even require this sort of communication. Not *all* donors require it, however. In fact, they are the exception.

I remain convinced that the most effective home visit is one in which the caller *listens* instead of speaks. We must remember that our mere presence makes a powerful statement. Yet this statement may be positive or negative. If the donor receives the message that we are really only interested in soliciting a pledge, our presence may convey a very negative message: "All they want is my money." However, if we are person-oriented and demonstrate a sincere interest in our brother or sister, we will have conveyed a very positive message indeed.

In *Megatrends,* John Naisbitt describes the world in which we live as "high tech." This depersonalized environment, says Naisbitt, creates a longing for "high touch." Persons need and seek a place where they are recognized as individuals and taken seriously as persons of worth. Our visit, then, is a magnificent opportunity to show our concern, not for their pledge, but for *them.* We can be certain that ours will be the only call the donor receives this week in which he or she is so affirmed as a person.

What, then, do our callers *say* when they make this visit? While the words may vary, the message is simply this: "How are you?"

Almost without exception, this question elicits the response: "I know we haven't been to church as frequently as we had expected to be. We've been (out of town a lot/sick/working Sundays)."

Notice that this response answers quite a different query from the one actually posed. Guilt and uneasiness drip from it like melting ice cream.

The caller has clearly failed to convey the message intended. It is not the caller's fault. It is the natural attempt by the host to justify what seems to him/her a wrong.

Ask the same question again—"How are you?" In fact, no matter what response is triggered, ask again and again until your host recognizes that you truly want to know *how he/she is.* If the caller can express this simple truth in a sincere manner, which prompts the host to reply to it *and actually begin to tell how he/she is,* the primary message of this visit will have been well delivered.

After the host has finished talking (this may take ten minutes or more), the caller may make a statement about the stewardship campaign. This statement should be upbeat and stress that the campaign is important. The host should then be asked if he/she has received a mailing from the church containing a pledge card. If the answer is affirmative, the caller might ask, "Will you be able to bring it to church this Sunday, or would it be more convenient for me to deliver it for you tonight?"

No matter what the response concerning the pledge, leave with a statement such as, "I'm glad we had this opportunity to get to know each other better. Hope to see you in church this Sunday."

What have we accomplished with such a call?

1. We have made it clear that we are members of the same church. It is the *donor's* church as well as the caller's.

2. We have removed any opportunity for the disgruntled to decry the fact that we "only come by when we want money."

3. We have presented the pledging opportunity in a low-pressure but positive way. The implication is that the donor will certainly pledge, the only question is how the card will be returned. This closing technique conveys a most positive message without being threatening.

4. Finally, we will have made a vital connection between the stewardship crusade and the evangelistic ministry of the church.

11. CALL ON EVERYONE—
NON-MEMBERS TOO!

How many members does your church have? How do you determine membership in the first place? Most churches have a substantial number of persons who, while not honest-to-goodness signed-on-the-line members, look to the church for services when they plan a wedding, funeral, reception, or other such event. To ignore these persons when planning your stewardship visitation is to overlook a significant amount of potential financial support. It is also to deny them an important component of religious affiliation. Whether you recognize it or not, your church is *their church* too.

Occasionally the argument is heard that we should ask for a commitment to Christ and the church first and ask for a financial commitment later. This will work for some persons. Most people, however, will respond in the reverse order. It is easier (and a lot more likely) to respond to an invitation to do something I already understand—visit church, work on a supper, make a financial contribution—than to respond to something so unique as a commitment to Jesus Christ.

T. K. Thompson reports a study done by the Board of Home Missions of the Congregational Christian Churches. Over a period of years it was discovered that churches received new members through *financial campaigns* for new buildings. The average number of new members received in this way was twenty-six. Maybe Jesus was right—"Where your treasure is, there your heart will be also."

When you prepare your lists for contacts, include everyone. List those who occasionally attend, who may be members of groups that meet in your building, whose children participate in your programming, who had a funeral service officiated by your pastor. Include everybody.

You may not realize a large financial gain from those persons initially, but you will be making an important statement to them. First of all you will be affirming them as persons worthy of acceptance into the Body of Christ. You will be pointing out to them that there are corresponding responsibilities associated with church affiliation. Finally you will be keeping the door open to them for further participation in the life of the church.

Don't rule people out before you even begin. Include them in.

12. HAVE A PRAYER VIGIL

Many congregations have discovered that an important part of their annual campaign is to undergird it with a prayer vigil. These vigils, which may vary in duration from twelve to seventy-two or more hours, provide a marvelous opportunity to integrate the spiritual life of the congregation with the financial commitment of the campaign. It is a way of saying that the spirituality of our members ultimately must be translated into their financial support and commitment for the ministry of the congregation in the coming year.

Larger congregations may wish to have the vigil divided by half-hour increments of time, while smaller congregations may require a one-hour commitment of those who keep the vigil. Whatever your local situation, you'll want to have on hand a quantity of materials to help persons center their thoughts and occupy their time in a creative and spiritually fulfilling manner. Of course, Bibles ought to be available, along with other devotional literature, but you might also want to consider having copies of the campaign literature highlighting the financial commitments to which you'll be asking persons to make their estimate. Depending upon the number of participants in the vigil, you will have an excellent opportunity to present your case at the very time when the donor is giving most prayerful consideration to his or her commitment to the church itself. (While some congregations have gone so far as to actually request the estimate card to be returned at the time of the vigil itself, I do not recommend this course, however.)

In the organizational chart for the Every Member commitment program you will see that one of the jobs is a prayer chairperson. The primary task of the prayer chairperson will be to organize the prayer vigil and any other devotional opportunities throughout the life of the campaign. The chairperson will very likely need some assistance to insure that all of the time slots are properly filled and that the persons who sign up are properly motivated.

PART TWO
Financial Administration

1. EVALUATE YOUR CONGREGATION'S GIVING POTENTIAL

Before you start the process of planning this year's financial campaign, ask your financial secretary to do a little homework for you. List the giving and pledge of each member family in the congregation in order of the size of the gift. Start with those who give absolutely nothing of record to the congregation and go all the way up to the highest giving family in the church. Then try to evaluate the breakdown of this giving pattern and determine the various percentages of your congregation that account for a given portion of income. Here we use the image of the pyramid to try to stratify the giving pattern of the congregation. Note that the top 3% will typically provide a quarter or 25% of the congregation's income. The next 10% similarly provides another 25% and then the next 20% accounts for the third quarter. The top 33%, therefore, accounts for as much as ¾ of the congregation's income. What this suggests, conversely, is that the bottom 67% produces only 25% of the revenue for your church. In fact, often 50% of the church provides less than 1% of total income.

Note that I have not suggested that these are ideals or even goals to be reached but rather indicators of how a typical congregation's giving pattern tends to appear. Your congregation, of course, will have its own particular pattern that would be appropriate for you, but note any substantial variances from these norms.

Particular care must be given to evaluate the top 3% of your givers. If they account for more than 25% of what you are receiving from the congregation at large, you are probably depending upon them too much and not working hard enough to develop the rest of your congregation's giving. If, however, they account for much less than 25% of your whole income, you'll need to work to begin to lift their sights. Many congregations would discover that the most efficient way of increasing total church income would be to work with these top donors in trying to increase their giving so that they might at least equal the 25% norm that most churches have already established.

There are, of course, exceptions to this rule and your congregation may be one of them, but that's not likely. Two exceptional congregations are an extremely homogeneous congregation, perhaps in a new and developing suburban community, or if you are an extraordinarily heterogeneous congregation made up of some very well-to-do folk and perhaps a substantial portion of members from lower economic backgrounds. If your church is really homogeneous, you may need to expand the top stratum from 3% to 5% or even more to discover your top 25%. On the other hand, if you are that rare heterogeneous congregation, you may reach the 25% threshold of total church income from the first 1% or 2%. The point of all this background evaluation and survey is to help you see where your efforts ought be directed in this year's campaign. If you have an under-performing stratum in your membership—perhaps that top 3% not giving the 25% that the norm would suggest or perhaps too narrow a gap between the next two 25% strata—you will then be able to identify where to expend your energies most efficiently. This does not suggest that we ignore the congregation at large but rather that we understand where corrective action needs to be taken so that we can most efficiently take that action at a given point in time.

An excellent way to determine what your congregation *might* be able to give is to determine what your people are giving now as a percentage of incomes. It is not necessary to ask your membership to tell you their incomes. Instead, assuming your congregation is representative of your community at large, use the Effective Buying Income figures for your community. These figures are published annually in a special July issue of *Sales and Marketing Management Magazine* (available in most libraries).

Effective Buying Income figures are published for every area in the U.S. with particular data for urban areas. EBI corresponds closely with "take-home" pay and gives a good approximation of what your donors have to give.

EBI is quoted by households, so you will probably need to convert your membership from "members" into households. If you know the number of family units in your congregation, use that; if not, multiply total membership by two-thirds. Next, multiply the number of households by the median Effective Buying Income (EBI) for your community, or urban neighborhood. This will approximate the total income of your congregation.

Calculate the total receipts for last year. Use all budgeted and special offerings. Now divide the total giving by the total congregational income figure. This will show you the percentage of income given to the church by your member families. (Don't be surprised if the percentage for your church seems low. It's not unusual to find giving at the 2% of EBI level.)

Here's how the computations might work in a typical congregation.

Sample United Protestant Church
East Cupcake, Michigan

1. Number of households—179

2. Medial EBI in Cupcake County—$21,692

3. Total income of congregation—(#1 × #2)—$3,882,868

4. 198 x total giving at Sample UMC—$88,642

5. Average giving per household (#4 ÷ #1)—$495.21

6. Average % of income (#5 ÷ #2)—2.28%

7. If each household increased giving by 1% of income, increased giving would total—$38,828

8. With the above increase in giving, our income for 199_ would be $127,471.

2. ONE SIZE DOESN'T FIT ALL

One of the frustrating things about finances in the church is that, as the hymn writer tells us, new occasions do teach new duties. The very thing that works so well at Church A typically is a colossal failure at Church B. In a profession like ministry, where pastors move from A to B and C to D, this moving target approach to church finances can be a real problem.

We can try to get the congregation to adapt to our style, to do it the way we did it in some other place. However, this is seldom a workable solution. There are more members than pastors. Clearly, if someone needs to do the changing, it's likely to be the leadership, the pastor.

A variety of styles of financial development needs to be available in each congregation. For those who prefer the discipline of weekly budgeted giving, a modified-unified budget style of church finance would be most helpful. For those who prefer the occasional special giving opportunity, that style needs also to be available. Similarly, any number of ongoing and intermediate campaigns are well received by some members of the congregation. We're describing a smorgasbord concept of church financial administration. Some of your members like to give weekly. Some don't. Some of your members give regularly. Some don't. Some of your members will consider planned giving. Others won't. Your financial style of administration ought to be reflective of a wide variety of tastes and a wide opportunity for Christian stewardship.

The Finance Committee is seldom a representative sample of the entire congregation. They are leaders, or they shouldn't be on the committee in the first place. Provide opportunities for giving that may not be the preferred methods of committee members. For example, it is not unusual for the leadership to be committed to a "unified budget" style of administration. In this pattern, second-mile requests or special offerings might be discouraged or even prohibited. When this is done, however, you are assuming that "one size fits all" and eliminating an important option for many members.

Your members are not all alike. Give opportunity for varieties of giving, and the church will give more. It's about as simple as that.

3. KNOW WHAT MOTIVATES YOUR DONORS

If we only knew all the things that donors *didn't* need to know, our visit would be a lot more comfortable. In fact it is probably our misconceptions about what donors want and need to know that gets in the way of much of the visitation process.

"My Associate here has a peachy idea for increasing the offering. Use reverse psychology and tell them we don't WANT their old money!"

In the traditional every member visitation program, the assumption has always seemed that the donors know little or nothing about the ministry and program of the church. A visitor's task is to bring them up to date. This indoctrination approach is primarily seen as motivation for increased giving. The result of such a call, however, is that it tends to be sales-oriented. Typically, this sales orientation is expressed by using the church budget or proposed church budget as the basic educational tool. We teach the people about the church by interpreting the church budget. Sometimes this type of interpretation is even creative and can occasionally be effective, but it nearly always misses the point.

A key learning for most of our visitors ought to be the fact that few of our donors are motivated to give by the church's need to receive. That is to say, donors seldom increase their giving by 10% because the local congregation's needs have increased 10%. Giving comes from a number of different motives, and these motives need to be explored so that we understand the proper context of our visit.

Donors are motivated by positive motives, such as gratitude, love, and joy. However negative motives also abound. Donors sometimes give out of feelings of guilt, out of desires for power and status, in opposition to a cause they oppose, and for a variety of other less than wholesome reasons. Over time, of course, the hope is that one can change and improve the motivation of our donors so that they tend to have more positive motives and goals. For the short term, however, this type of training and improvement is unlikely to occur.

What this implies to our visitor, however, is that it is not necessary to sell the budget, and it is not necessary to motivate the donor. Understand that the donor is likely to have a number of personal and already existing motives which are the ones that will make the difference in that person's gift to the church in the coming year.

The goal of this year's visit, therefore, is to enhance the donor's attitude toward the church and to deliver this one basic message: The church cares about its members. Our presence there delivers that message much more eloquently than any words that we might use. Once the visitor understands that the message has already been delivered, a good deal of the pressure has been removed and the visitor can get about the business of trying to listen rather than to speak.

4. ALL DONORS ARE NOT CREATED EQUAL

One of the most difficult lessons for me to learn was that local church finance committees seldom understand the membership at large. Like so many of us, the typical member of the finance committee assumes that most persons are just like him/her. If the committee members are giving at a sacrificial level, they also perceive that everyone else is giving equally sacrificially. Such is seldom the case, however.

Perhaps it would help if we realized that all donors do not give out of the same perspective or motivation. Robert Sharpe, of the National Planned Giving Institute, highlights four types of givers.

1. *The Impulsive Giver*—By far the most common sort. May respond to any solicitation if she or he is in the mood or may reject if not in the mood. This donor will give, but only when asked. The key for these persons, therefore, is to *ask* over and over again.

Some impulse givers may make a pledge, but it is crucial to realize that this pledge is only an "impulse," a statement of intention at one point in time, not forever. We will need to work with impulse donors all year long if they are to sustain their pledge.

More likely, however, is the possibility that impulsive givers will not pledge. Remembering that impulsive donors have difficulty sustaining a pledge anyway, this is less a problem than you might expect. What this donor type needs is a regular opportunity for giving. Special offerings and other targeted giving solicitations often meet the needs of impulsive givers.

2. *The Habitual Giver*—Although there are habitual givers to all charities, the church probably has more than anybody else. These givers seem to like the pledge system inasmuch as it allows them to establish the routine which feels most comfortable. Conversely, habitual givers do not respond well to special offering appeals.

A strategy which may appeal to these donors is to establish "Donor Clubs" or other plans for regular giving. Perhaps you could develop groups of "Mission Partners," "Christian Education Associates," or a similar cadre of persons who need the discipline of good habits.

3. *The Thoughtful Giver*—An excellent donor resource although com-

prising only about 7% of all donors. These persons give thoughtfully (and generously!) to projects they understand and support. These givers are frequently the ones most influenced by your "case" or promotional efforts.

Thoughtful givers often make the largest contribution to capital fund campaigns and other occasional efforts. Yet the largess is far from spontaneous. Thoughtful donors require an effective development process, including a statement of need, motivation, and an opportunity for response.

4. *The Careful Giver*—The smallest donor group but may provide more gifts than any other category. Only approximately 3% of all donors, careful givers, nevertheless, give out of a plan for distribution. Stewardship may be the primary motive as well as estate planning, tax avoidance, and efficient distribution.

Virtually the opposite of impulsive donors, careful givers are not much influenced by special appeals. Funds given for emergencies or other occasional offerings tend to come from a discretionary giving fund which the donor has already established (at least in his/her mind).

The bottom line for financial leaders, therefore, is to understand the widely divergent giving motives and styles of today's donors. No one strategy is likely to fit the needs of every group. Instead, a variety of commitment and giving opportunities must be developed to allow for these individual differences.

5. RECHANNEL
COMMITMENTS

First Church had a problem. Relentlessly, like the ticking of a clock, the building debt retirement fund was nearing the pay-off point. In less than a year the mortgage would be paid and, presumably, the level of giving would be substantially reduced.

What's the problem? It surely does not lie in the simple need of the church to receive more money from its members. Nor is it rooted in additional building plans or needs. The problem lies instead in the need of the membership to retain a focused, intentional level of stewardship.

If the funds currently being received by the congregation for the building fund are legitimate, then a similar amount could be allocated for another purpose. To retain the current challenge level of giving, the congregation will need to address several issues:

1. The current level of giving proves a potential for giving beyond the basic budget. While many may have denied the possibility of the current giving pace, the facts prove the resources are there.

2. Because the giving to the building fund is designated only for building debt retirement, the membership has the right to reduce their giving correspondingly when the debt is discharged.

3. If the giving level increased substantially because of the challenge of the building program, a similar increase may be possible through a challenge of another project.

4. An intentional effort to capture the interest of current building fund donors could very well succeed in rechannelling their commitment to another project or ministry.

5. The time is right to survey these donors to discover their interests and concerns. Expressed interests are those most likely to find ready support.

You will, of course, frequently hear the opinion that an interim period (a rest?) between projects is preferable. There is little evidence to support this contention, however. It is more likely the point of view of an indolent human nature whose natural response to any challenge is resistance.

Our task as leaders in the church is *to lead,* not to follow the path of least resistance. The need for sacrificial giving is a challenge rooted in the essential nature of an incomplete church in an imperfect world. Just as we mustn't promise at the beginning of a campaign that we will never ask again, we similarly need not halt the momentum of a successful project out of a naive desire for respite.

6. THE A.F.I. METHOD—ASK FOR IT

It is amazing how many ministries are never initiated, how many gifts are never received, how many dollars are never given just because nobody ever asked for them. Is there something you need? *Ask For It!* Is there something you want? *Ask For It!* There is no secret here, no particular genius. Have a need? Ask for help. Got a problem? Tell people. Something you need? Tell folks what they can do to help.

A church group with which I was consulting seemed unusually resistant to any suggestion of a direct mail solicitation. "Do you realize how many fund-raising requests our people get all the time?" a member asked me. "What kind of response are we likely to get when we will be competing with so many others?" The answer, although imprecise, seems utterly obvious—"a lot more than if we don't ask at all."

Check out what Matthew 7:7 and James 4:2 have to say about this. The Bible expresses what we already ought to know—we have a right (and a need!) to ask for any legitimate need. Use the A.F.I. method and you will find success in fund-raising.

7. HOW MANY STATEMENTS ARE ENOUGH?

It is a tragic irony that the I.R.S. saw the relevance of statements long before stewardship leaders did. Originally the statements of receipt given to donors were merely to acknowledge a gift, usually for tax purposes.

"Dear Mr. Gribner: We would like to thank you for bringing your pledge payments up to date. We certainly would LIKE to thank you. Sincerely . . .' "

The *real* function of statements today, however, is to remind the donor of his/her giving and whether it is current with the accrued pledged amount. Annual statements, while still valid as a receipt, are unable to provide much help in encouraging currency by the donor. Quarterly statements are better but still inadequate to do the job properly.

Today's adult population is geared to one financial phenomenon which determines all others. *Monthly payments* are the facts of financial life for people today. The charitable giving dollar is competing with all the other spending opportunities in the life of the donor. If you only send a quarterly reminder, you will be in competition with creditors who send monthly statements. Who do you think will get the better response?

It is more work to send statements on a monthly basis, of course. There will also be increased costs associated with postage, envelopes, and (when paid staff is involved) wages. The net result, however, is increased giving, more regular cash flow, and a marvelous opportunity for regular communication and stewardship promotion.

Many congregations are discovering the wisdom of using monthly statements as a vehicle for mailing the next month's offering envelopes. You will avoid the trap of purchasing envelopes you don't need. You will make a powerful statement when the envelopes arrive each month. You may add special offering envelopes and promotional literature for occasional emphases. The key is timeliness. Keep it current and future-oriented. The statement is history, but its result is a future response.

In addition to the statement itself and the regular offering envelopes, your monthly mailing should include at least two other pieces. The first is a report from the finance committee telling what was done with last month's gift. (See II.18 "Financial Reporting—What Did You Get? What Did You Do with It?") Finally, don't forget to include a return envelope. While it is true that you wish to invite donors to *bring* their gifts, remember that one of the functions of the monthly statement is to help donors remain current. One way for many to accomplish this is to mail any arrearage when the statement arrives.

If you are skeptical about the value of monthly statements, test them for a year with donors who traditionally fall behind. Announce that you are prepared to offer a monthly statement to anyone who requests one or anyone "whose share-giving pattern suggests it would be helpful." Our experience shows that monthly statements don't "cost," they pay off with increased giving and dramatically increased enthusiasm as persons stay current all year long.

8. SETTING TARGETS FOR GOOD GIVING

The rangy center had been a great scorer in high school, but his freshman year had been a disaster. He never seemed to get the ball. Over the summer he worked on one technique and once again discovered the scoring touch. The technique? An uplifted hand gave the guard a target to aim for. The ball tends to go where it has a target, a reason for being there.

Church people need targets too. An "offering" will get some response, but a goal tells people what you want from them. If the usual offering generates $500 for a special project, a $1,000 goal tells people you need double the usual gift. One rather simple administrative cure for poor giving is to try to set a proper target. The easiest thing that works is to stress *weekly* giving. Yet many are the pledge cards that offer three, four, and sometimes even more giving options. Weekly, monthly, quarterly, annually, and any number of other alternatives only cloud the issue. What we want to encourage is that donors *bring,* not send, their gifts.

What will happen if donors insist on some other type of payment option other than weekly? They will probably end up paying the way they want. Our task, however, is not to tell them how they can or cannot give but rather to set a higher target, or a proper strategy for their giving practices. Weekly works.

But there are other methods of setting a helpful target to improved giving by your donors. Below are three strategies which are proven to work in many different situations.

---

1. SHOW HOW GIVING MAKES A DIFFERENCE.

People need to know what you expect from them. Do you want a big gift or a smaller one? What difference will their giving make? There must be a "contingent dimension" to every gift—something will happen if a gift is made that will not occur if no gift is made. For example, "Each $5.00 will enable 20 children to be vaccinated for tuberculosis," shows the donor what will happen if $5.00 is contributed and, correspondingly, what will not happen if no gift is made.

When presenting your annual campaign materials, it is important to include this "contingent dimension" as well. If your goal is increased giving, show what will happen if giving is increased or what the impact of level giving will be.

2. SHOW HOW EACH DONOR'S GIVING COMPARES
WITH OTHERS.

Successful churches have one thing in common—leaders who are willing to lead. Financially speaking, leaders are important, too. Lyle Schaller has observed that every church has at least five persons who think they are the top giver in the congregation (even though only one of them actually is the leading giver). I would venture that an additional three or four persons ought to be the leading giver. What can you do to raise the sights of these top-potential donors?

At least annually you should publish the giving records of every donor of record from the highest to the bottom. Remove all names, of course, but print the complete list. This will be the most helpful target many of your people will ever see. Several highly motivated persons will see how much their giving must be increased to become a leading donor; others will see how they compare to their peers. This is a virtually risk-free strategy, since top givers seldom reduce their giving upon discovering that others give less but many persons do give more when they are shown the giving of others. Try something like this.

It may be helpful in considering your family's estimate of giving for 199X to know the pattern of regular giving of our members during 199Y.

```
 1 Family gave $4,680—$90 per week
 2 Families gave $4,160—$80 per week
 2 Families gave $3,500—$70 per week
 3 Families gave $3,000-3,499—$60 + per week
 3 Families gave $2,500-2,999—$50 + per week
 8 Families gave $2,000-2,400—$40 + per week
 9 Families gave $1,500-1,999—$30 + per week
10 Families gave $1,300—$25 per week
 9 Families gave $1,000-1,299—$20 + per week
11 Families gave $780-999—$15 + per week
12 Families gave $520-779—$10 + per week
21 Families gave $260-519—$5-$10 per week
16 Families gave $100-259—$2-$5 per week
12 Families gave $1.00 per week or less
```

3. TELL DONORS A SUGGESTED AMOUNT TO CONSIDER.

Many donors will greet your solicitation with a blank stare because they haven't the slightest idea what you really want. You will be doing them and your cause a favor if you can suggest a target amount to "consider."

I once canvassed our block for the March of Dimes. Hardly anybody refused to give, but most gave only a dollar, a token amount. My last call was a new neighbor, a funeral director living in a residential neighborhood for the first time in his life. He legitimately wanted to know what we wanted from him. "What's the usual gift?" he asked. Swallowing hard, I responded, "$25.00!" Imagine my feeling when he fetched his checkbook and wrote out a check for exactly $25.00! "Thanks," I said, "You're the first guy on our block to give the 'usual' gift."

The point is that it was just as easy for him to give $25 as $1; the difference was the target.

9. SHARES—FAIR AND OTHERWISE

A critical question our people ask every time we make a financial appeal is "What should *I* give?" The implication is that there is an amount that is appropriate for each member of the organization.

Consider selling "shares" in your project. Calculate the cost of the project divided into a representative number of shares. This becomes your product, and your appeal becomes the selling of these shares.

For example, a new piano for the parlor costs $2,200. One hundred shares would cost $22 each. (You may wish to offer 200 shares at $11 each.) This provides a minimum gift within the reach of most of your givers and also suggests that some need to consider buying more than one share. (See the entry "Setting Targets for Good Giving," p. 44.)

The advantages of shares are:

1. It raises the basic gift amount. You will still get some $1.00 contributions for "the piano fund," but most gifts will come in multiples of $22.00.

2. It encourages persons to see their gift as a significant part of the whole. Particularly with pledges, the giver sees the importance of his/her gift. If a share is not subscribed, the project will not be complete.

3. It suggests that wealthier or more committed givers see the need to express their gift, not in multiples of dollars, but in multiples of shares. It is crucial for those who really want a new piano to realize that they need to pay the share of another member for whom the piano is not a priority.

Things to avoid in selling shares are:

1. The "Fair Share" suggestion that anything less is somehow not acceptable. Gifts in true proportion to ability are always welcome.

2. The implication that one share is all anyone need consider. "If we all would pay an additional $25, the debt would be retired," the finance chairman declared. Most people took him seriously and wrote out a check for $25 immediately, but some folks gave nothing. The result was a significant shortfall because those who could and should have given more were led to believe that $25 was what was expected of them. It is simply a fact that few congregations are composed of persons with equal abilities

or commitments. The "faithful few" will continue to carry the burden, but subscribing shares helps them calculate how.

Shares will work for more than pianos. Try them for missions projects, scholarships, choir robes, or most any good purpose. Persons *want* to share. Let them *have* a share.

10. DEAD HORSES *VS.* LIVE PROJECTS

"Two weeks from today we will have a special offering to get out of the hole," the finance committee chairperson announced. "We just haven't been receiving enough in recent weeks to cover our expenses. As it stands now, we are over $2,000 in the red. If we all give a little extra in this special offering, we will be able to start the summer with no deficit."

This ritual will be enacted in hundreds of congregations each spring. To pay off a budget deficit, a special offering is taken. Sometimes this is called "Catch-Up Sunday," "Budget Booster," a variation on the same theme. In each case, a crucial mistake is made.

Persons in these churches are invited to pay for a dead horse. Ministries completed but not yet paid for have little power to warm the blood or inspire the imagination. It is little wonder that these offerings seldom raise large sums and even more seldom create much enthusiasm. Dead horses are not much fun to pay for.

Why not place the emphasis upon future ministries? However difficult it may be to present it as exciting, almost any future program or ministry will be easier to sell than a completed one. Make the orientation a future ministry, fund it with the same special offering, and results should improve 20-50%.

Two churches faced virtually identical dilemmas as they entered the fall season. Each was nearly $2,000 behind budget pace for the year, with weekly offerings averaging about $900. One church received a "Catch-Up Sunday" offering and raised an additional $1,800 beyond the typical Sunday receipts.

The other congregation, however, targeted several of the fall's ministries and announced that several of these vital programs could not be assured unless adequate funding was received by a target date. On the same day that the first church was receiving its "Catch-Up" $1,800, this congregation's offering for future ministries totaled $7,700.

By guaranteeing funding for future ministries in advance, you will not need to expend subsequent receipts for these programs and can instead pay off any arrearage. The difference in attitude, you will notice, lies in what your donors understand themselves to be doing—financing important future ministries or paying for a dead horse.

11. THE "PROTECTION" DONORS DON'T NEED

Remember the old story about the boy who was late for school? The teacher asked why, and the lad replied, "I was helping an old lady cross the street." "For half an hour?" the teacher asked. "She didn't want to go," the boy responded.

"Help" is sometimes not only unnecessary, but it's occasionally even inappropriate. One prime example of inappropriate "help" is the common ploy of the pastor who tries to protect the people of the congregation. "Our people are already giving generously. We can't ask them to do any more," the pastor states. I am often tempted to ask if the pastor has any idea what the people are giving, generously or not. (But I usually resist the temptation.)

In fact nobody knows how much more the congregation would give if only they were asked. (See the A.F.I. Method, II.6.) Faithful laypersons continue to testify, "Why didn't someone tell us about these needs before?" The people of God want to do what is right. They need no protection from the truth.

Often the pastor or finance committee has an arbitrary number of appeals in mind, above which they will not go. "We can't have another special offering," they protest. Yet no one will ever know who would have responded and appreciated the opportunity, if only they had known about the need.

Some helpful rules for evaluating the appropriateness of a financial need or offering:

1. The cause must be related to the church or its ministry. It is a dangerous precedent to allow outside groups to solicit funds as part of the church. Resist the temptation to allow announcements concerning Boy Scout Bake Sales and the like. As a compromise, designate an area where non-member groups may solicit gifts, sell tickets, etc.

2. When there is a legitimate need, tell the people. Keep the emphasis positive and upbeat, but tell them.

3. Use low-key solicitation. Recognize that not every project will enjoy the support of every member. Make it voluntary.

4. Establish the precedent that it is acceptable to say "No" to any particular asking. You will not get far by stressing the loyalty motive.

5. Make all-purpose offering envelopes readily available. This eliminates the problem of how to get the funds to the right place. Just have donors mark the envelope with the proper designation and place it in the regular offering plate.

6. Establish realistic limitations upon the number of times a project may be announced and solicited. Usually two weeks is optimum. Anything less comes as a surprise, and more frequent appeals suffer from diminishing returns.

7. Consider more closely targeting potential donors. Not every need must come before the entire congregation. Some projects will have a natural "market" which could be solicited without a church-wide appeal.

12. STRESS STEWARDSHIP— NOT NEEDS

Wesley Church was completely frustrated. They had worked like crazy trying to show the membership all the needs of the church. They had used every medium they could think of to demonstrate why the 9% increase in the budget was absolutely necessary. Yet they had fallen 4% short of their pledged goals. "This must be a bad time for fund-raising," the stewardship chairperson said as she prefaced her report.

Down the road at Asbury Church a low-key pledge campaign had gone "over the top" with the largest increase in Asbury's history. "This has been the most fun of any stewardship campaign we've ever done," reported Bob of the stewardship committee.

Two similar congregations, two different stories; what made the difference? Note the subtle differences in the reporting. Wesley Church had engaged in *fund-raising* while Asbury clearly conducted a *stewardship campaign.* There is a difference.

Fund-raising will experience success or failure depending upon several factors:

1. The relative prosperity of the donors
2. The attractiveness of the project
3. The skill or enthusiasm of the solicitors
4. The degree of interpretation of the project

Stewardship, however, is rooted in the donor's need to give, irrespective of the apparent needs of the congregation to receive. Thus the emphasis is not upon the budget or its component line items, but rather upon the donor's response to God's gracious gifts. Instead of saying, "Here's what we're trying to do; here's how much we need; how much will you give?" the stewardship approach would ask, "How much of your income are you ready to give to God for the work of the church?"

The difference between these two approaches must not be underestimated. It is the difference described by saying, "Don't think of your giving in terms of *for what* but in terms of *to Whom.*"

13. PUSH PERCENTAGES— PROPORTIONATE GIVING

Someone has defined stewardship simply as "living *on purpose*." It is the *purposefulness* that is at the heart of any successful church finance program.

We must help persons understand their giving in terms of its percentage of their income. Not only is this biblical, but also it is absolutely essential if we are to move beyond "fund-raising" toward true stewardship.

The best known example of proportionate giving is the tithe. However, the disparity between the *concept* of giving 10% and the *practice* of giving 2-3% is well documented. If we are to help our membership properly evaluate its stewardship, we must use proportionate giving as an instrument.

Use the following tables to show your givers where they stand in terms of percentage of income. Encourage them to increase their giving by a percent of income per year.

An increase in giving of 1% of one's income will seem reasonable to your donors, even though the dollar amount might be equivalent to a 50% increase. Hold firm to the "growth in giving" suggestion, however. The entire point of this strategy is to break out of a dollar-oriented response and encourage proportionate stewardship.

The recent Rockefeller Foundation study, "The Charitable Behavior of Americans," endorses the merits of this strategy. The study documents that church attenders who pledge give twice the amount of non-pledgers, and that pledgers who express their commitment as a percentage of income give nearly three times the amount of non-pledgers.

> Non-pledging churchgoers $440
> Pledgers pledging $ amounts—$880
> Pledgers committing %—$1,240

Encourage proportionate giving and you will be accomplishing two worthy purposes at the same time. First, you will be helping your members to practice a more intentional level of stewardship, but in addition you will be raising more money for your ministries.

CHURCH GIVING CALCULATOR

WEEKLY INCOME	2%	3%	4%	5%	6%	7%	8%	9%	10%	15%
$ 100.00	$ 2	$ 3	$ 4	$ 5	$ 6	$ 7	$ 8	$ 9	$ 10	$ 15
$ 200.00	4	6	8	10	12	14	16	18	20	30
$ 300.00	6	9	12	15	18	21	24	27	30	45
$ 400.00	8	12	16	20	24	28	32	36	40	60
$ 500.00	10	15	20	25	30	35	40	45	50	75
$ 600.00	12	18	24	30	36	42	48	54	60	90
$ 700.00	14	21	28	35	42	49	56	63	70	105
$ 800.00	16	24	32	40	48	56	64	72	80	120
$ 900.00	18	27	36	45	54	63	72	81	90	135
$1000.00	20	30	40	50	60	70	80	90	100	150
$1100.00	22	33	44	55	66	77	88	99	110	165
$1200.00	24	36	48	60	72	84	96	108	120	180
$1500.00	30	45	60	75	90	105	120	135	150	225

14. INCOME INCREASE MATRIX

It is wise periodically to refresh our memories concerning ways in which an actual increase in cash receipts may be realized through the pledge system. Note that the only meaningful figure is cash *received,* not pledged. The "income increase matrix" shows the dynamics required for any increase to occur.

In the matrix grid, the horizontal line refers to an increase in percentage of pledge actually paid. The vertical represents an increase in the pledged amount itself. Any increase in either category will result in an increase in cash receipts as long as the other figure also increases or remains unchanged.

For example, assume Mr. and Mrs. Donor made a pledge last year of $10.00 per week ($520 annually) yet paid only 80% of their pledge, $8.00 per week or $416 for the year. This year the Donors have increased their pledge to $12.50, a 25% increase. If their payment percentage remains unchanged (80%), the actual cash received by the church will be $10.00 per week or $520 for the year. This same cash increase could be realized by a corresponding 25% increase in percentage of pledge actually paid. Thus the $8.00 amount is increased by 25% and becomes $10.00 weekly or $520 annually.

The INCOME INCREASE MATRIX shows how gain is achieved by increasing the pledge itself or the percentage paid.

Payment %

Pledge Amount

Note that either event will produce the same net result, an increase of 25% in cash received. Thus the potential strategies for achieving the

increase are anything that will produce an increase in the amount
pledged *or* anything that will result in a higher percentage of the pledge
being paid.

It should be apparent that increasing both categories will produce the
greatest increase. A 25% increase in the pledge of $10.00 becomes $12.50
and a 25% increase in payment percentage results in receipts of 100% of
$12.50 or $12.50 weekly, $650 annually—an increase of 56%!

The goal of a successful stewardship program will be those strategies
which increase amounts pledged, percentages of pledges paid, or both.
Some donors will respond better to one technique while others prefer the
opposite. Work on *both* strategies throughout the year. Use the matrix to
evaluate your plan. Does it include motivations for more than merely
pledging? Do you help your donors evaluate their payment performance?
Put both techniques to work this year.

15. BARRETT'S LAW

Sometimes the solutions to problems are so obvious that we look right past them. Remember the old story about the smuggler who crossed the border every day between Juarez and El Paso? Each day he would approach customs pushing a wheelbarrow filled with straw. The agents were naturally suspicious of such a load and never failed to examine the straw with great diligence, but to no avail. Ultimately one agent promised amnesty if only the smuggler would tell *what* he was smuggling and how he was doing it. Imagine the agent's chagrin when the fellow announced that he was smuggling . . . wheelbarrows!

Such an incredibly obvious relationship exists between contributions to the church and worship attendance that we seldom note the strategic opportunities it affords. Yet the greatest percentage increases in giving come, not from those who significantly increase the *amount* they put in the offering plate, but from those who put offerings in the plate more *frequently.*

Since few persons indeed would ever attend worship and put nothing in the offering, the truth of Barrett's Law should be beyond dispute. Barrett's Law declares, "When they park it in the pew they plop it in the plate."

This banal little aphorism ought to suggest that attendance-increasing strategies are actually fund-raising strategies. Whatever causes less active members to become more active will have the inevitable result of raising revenue along with consciousness.

As we examine potential attendance-boosting activities, we should remember that good stewardship becomes a means as well as an end. Stewardship may be seen as a barometer indicating levels of spiritual vitality. We encourage good stewardship because it is a means toward achieving and maintaining spiritual health. I particularly like Ashley Hale's statement that "the aim of stewardship development is not to finance the church's annual operating budget but to change lives."

Yet it was Jesus who probably said it best: "Where your treasure is, there will your heart be also" (Matthew 6:21).

16. DESIGNATED GIVING

It started in the late 1960s. Movie theaters across the country began to offer two, three, four, and more screens. Along with this change came the phenomenon of choosing which film to see. Now it is an unusual theater which does not offer patrons at least two choices. During this fifteen-year period ticket prices have quadrupled with little market resistance. Moviegoers are willing to pay $3.00-$6.00 to get in the theater—but they reserve the right to "pick the flick."

The church, however, moves in a different direction. The Unified Budget, once the exception, now is the rule in Protestant congregations. Donors are encouraged to "buy the entire package." Often this brings resistance and skepticism. Should we be surprised?

Imagine our reaction if the ushers at the movies began to behave like church finance committees. We pay our $8.00 with some ambivalence but look forward to seeing *E.T.*. When we reach our seat, however, we discover that the management has decided to show us *Das Boot* instead. Maybe we even like *Das Boot*. No matter. Our enthusiasm begins to wane. *We* like to make the decisions about what we get for *our* money.

This is not a recent phenomenon. The North American Inter-Church Stewardship Survey of 1971 indicated that two thirds of laity favored designated giving opportunities. (Two thirds of clergy opposed!) Yet, in spite of the mandate, designated giving opportunities today are the exception.

What happens when people are given a chance to direct their gift to a particular ministry or choose between several ministry options? The response I have observed in church after church is that giving increases—sometimes drastically.

I know a congregation which raises nearly as much money for missions and hunger ministries as it does for everything else. How do they do it? They work at it; of this there can be no doubt. Their strategy, however, is to rely upon designated giving opportunities.

I have seen congregations give members an occasional Sunday on which their offering may be designated for a particular ministry or category of ministry (missions, education, building, etc.) with outstanding success. A small town congregation chose designated giving as the vehicle to ask for second-mile giving to its budget. Where typical weekly income was averaging $450, the day for designated giving received $5,542! The critical ingredient? Designation.

Some people love smorgasbords. Some don't. Some church folks like to fund all the programs and ministries of their church through a single pledge. *Some don't.* You will find that enthusiasm for your programs will be at a higher level and *you will receive more money* if you show that you trust the people. Give them a chance to put the money where they want it to go. Try designated giving. (See Second Chance Sunday, p. 75.)

17. CHURCH CASH MANAGEMENT

A basic stewardship responsibility, which is often overlooked by church treasurers, is the management of cash between the time of receipt and disbursement. Just as much as endowment funds, these monies deserve good management techniques to assure that they accomplish the maximum.

Cash management is not really something new to be added; *all* churches practice it. The only question is whether the practice will be *good* cash management or not. The simple matter of receiving cash or checks in the Sunday offering presents a management opportunity. Our goal will be to get the most ministry for the money. Here are four strategies to help you get the most from whatever cash resources you may have.

1. Establish a cash flow budget. Recognize that your money will not come in in 52 equal offerings. Christmas and Lent offerings are likely to be high, while July and August are often shockingly low. Similarly, expenses cannot always be spread evenly throughout the year. Utilities, insurance, maintenance, and many other regular expenses are not always evenly incurred.

It is not a difficult matter to establish accounts for these expenses. Simply transfer 8-10% of the budgeted totals for each of these items to the designated account each month. Even when there are no expenses for this particular item this month (insurance, for example), 8-10% of the annual budgeted amount should be transferred. Then, when the large bill comes due, funds will be ready to pay it without resorting to last year's cash management tactic—robbing Peter to pay Paul.

2. Put cash flow money to work. It is not enough to hold money until it's ready to be spent. Good stewardship suggests that these funds can work even while waiting. Money should be invested *someplace* at all times. No one knows how many dollars languish in low-interest or non-interest bearing accounts in churches all across the land. It has been my observation that it is not unusual to find congregations with 10-20% of their annual budget deposited in a checking account at any given time.

Consider this simple strategy. Categorize the types of cash funds your church holds. In general, nearly every congregation will have long-term, short-term, and current funds on hand at all times. Match these funds to investment options which parallel their maturity potential. Permanent or long-term funds can be invested in certificates of deposit or bonds with longer maturities and corresponding high returns. Short-term funds can be invested in 90- or 180-day investments. Even current cash can be put to work with good cash management.

Consider using a money market mutual fund for current cash income. Each week the offering is deposited in the account. Monies earn higher yields than bank savings accounts. Monthly bills are scheduled for payment on the same date each month. A single check is written on the mutual fund account to cover the total of all bills to be paid. (Interest continues until the check clears.) This check is then deposited in your regular checking account and the bills paid in the traditional way. Congregations using this system have achieved increased income of from 1% to 3% of their annual budgets.

3. Take advantage of discounts, but make certain they are *real* discounts. Discounts for quantity purchases are fine, provided: a) the commodity is what you will use, b) the commodity will not decompose or become unusable, and c) the discount is better than the return on investment otherwise available to you.

Without computing a formal present value tabulation, it is relatively easy to estimate when a discount is a real discount. For example, let us assume that you have a regular linen service contract for mops and cleaning rags which costs $10.00 per month. The service notifies you that you are eligible for a 5% discount if you prepay your total $120 annual contract. Is this a good deal? You are, in effect, loaning the vendor money at 5%. You can earn better than this with any investment option. You will then reject this "discount" option.

What about the common "2/10 net 30" discount available through many vendors? If a 5% discount is not worth considering, what about a 2%? A crucial distinction should be noticed here—the 2% discount is not for an entire year, it is for *20 days,* the difference between the tenth day (the last day the 2% discount is available) and the thirtieth day (the last day the net/full price is available before carrying charges are added). The actual discount on an annual basis may be computed this way:

$$2/10 \text{ net } 30 = 2\% \times \frac{360 \text{ days}}{20 \text{ days}} = 2\% \times 18 = 36\%$$

The actual discount, on an annual basis, is *36%!* You cannot afford to miss this discount. Another way to view this common transaction is to assume that the goods really cost 98% of the invoice price. If you elect not to pay within the 10-day cash period you will be assessed, in effect, a 36% annual penalty for late payment.

4. Get the best interest rate on invested funds. Once upon a time there seemed to be only two types of investment—safe ones with low interest, and risky ones with high interest. Today this distinction has been blurred substantially. While risk and return are still related, many excellent investment opportunities are available which offer good yields without exposure to significant market risk.

Certificates of deposit are available everywhere and pay a premium over passbook or statement savings in return for the loss of liquidity. Numerous money market funds offer better returns with little risk because the diversification possible through funds of this size reduces market risk exposure.

Don't assume that higher returns necessarily mean great risk. I know of no church that has lost a penny through investing in money markets and similar devices. Check it out. It's only good stewardship to get the most out of your cash.

18. FINANCIAL REPORTING— WHAT DID YOU GET? WHAT DID YOU DO WITH IT?

The development process doesn't end when the gift is received. Of course, you will want to say "Thank you" to your donors in a variety of ways. In addition to thanking the donor, however, it is important to report two important outcomes.

1. Tell how much the offering receipts were for the project, i.e., "Over $240 was received through the Camp Sunday offering." If you had a goal in mind, tell whether or not you reached it. If this was the largest camp offering ever, why not say so? It is amazing how many offerings are announced and promoted but never reported. It is as if the offering had never been received.

2. Next, tell what was done or accomplished with the money. The donor is vitally interested in hearing what difference his or her gift made. It is nice to know that more than $240 was received through the camp offering, but it is much more satisfying to hear that these gifts enabled six children to experience a total of 260 hours of Christian education experiences at camp. Next year the donors will remember that their gift did more than become a number in a report; it became a bridge that enabled kids to receive an important experience.

3. Have someone who benefited from the offering say, "Thank you." It's nice when the finance leaders express gratitude, but the most powerful feedback comes when a direct beneficiary says, "Thanks." Children, particularly, are effective in this role. Teach them to thank their benefactors.

19. THE "SALT BLOCK"
METHOD

It is a frustrating fact of lore that horses can be led to water but not made to drink. Yet the wise rider knows that a stop at the salt block on the way to the stream often results in the desired outcome. This suggests that the church needs to provide the proper experiences if certain outcomes are expected.

For instance, wills and bequests are not commonly understood by young-adult families, nor are they high on the list of felt needs. However, young adults turn out in droves for seminars on inflation-fighting and other consumer economic topics. Why not schedule such an event and simply include some estate planning information as a part of it? You'll have their attention, and family finances is a marvelous context in which to discuss estate planning.

Senior citizens and middle-aged adults demonstrate considerable interest in planning for retirement. Estate planning could easily become an important part of such a pre-retirement seminar.

Rather than waste time promoting events that have only marginal interest, learn to build on those proven winners that pull the crowds. Most anything worth doing is worth its "salt."

20. DON'T BE AFRAID OF DEBT

Many churches are dead and don't even know it. Time after time church leaders tell me that they are having a difficult time raising operating revenues. "But thank goodness we have no debt." This is a revealing statement about the way most churches operate. To be "free and clear" is the goal. What about the goal of winning persons to Christ? What about the goal of a growing, dynamic congregation? What about the goal of all those ministries you would initiate if you had the money?

Debt, while occasionally seen as the enemy, is either good or bad. Debt can be an oppressive burden but can also be the bridge to an exciting and vital future. What makes the difference?

We must understand what debt is and does if we are to utilize it creatively.

In his book, *Your Church Has Real Possibilities,* Robert Schuller lists three principles for borrowing money:

1. Never borrow to the extent that it will whittle away your net worth. Your net worth must always be growing, so as to provide a sound financial base on which to operate.

2. Never borrow money to pay for interest on debt. Before you increase your corporate debt, broaden your financial base to demonstrate a regular cash flow that can at least pay for the added interest cost of the proposed increased debt.

3. Never borrow more than you can amortize over a 20-year period. This provides an adequate time frame during which you can complete these growth projects needed to sustain enthusiasm and yet have a realistic prospect of eventually paying off all indebtedness.

In addition to these three borrowing principles, Schuller makes two more significant points about debt.

A good capital project can realistically be expected to generate additional income to pay off the principal of the loan. For example, you need $100,000 to complete a parking lot offering 140 new parking spaces. The interest on the debt is $12,000 per year. This is the amount your current congregation will need to pay. The new lot should generate new members sufficient to pay off the principal ($100,000) within the note period.

"Debt consciousness and the fear of debt can kill a church," Schuller continues. Needed improvements, additions, and programs deferred because of debt will likely never be completed. If debt is a good enough reason to defer a project today, we may be assured that some other reason will be found to torpedo the project in the future.

In summary, debt properly administered can be the financial catalyst for dynamic growth. It can be a powerful statement to the membership and newcomers that this congregation is intentional about the ministries it wishes to provide. Debt can break out of limiting circumstances by providing the enabling factors necessary for success. Don't be afraid of debt.

"WHAT'S NEW ABOUT TIGHT MONEY? IT'S ALWAYS BEEN
TIGHT AROUND HERE."

21. PRE-PAYING PLEDGES

The summer doldrums—the bane of many a finance committee. Attendance drops and with it goes the cash flow. There are people, of course, who do not intend to give to the church when they don't attend, but most people really do pledge for the full 52 weeks. They pledge but they don't pay. What can you do about it?

Encouraging people to prepay a portion of their summer pledge in May makes sense for at least four reasons:

REV. TWEEDLE, D.D.

©CHAS.CARTWRIGHT

"I just said we were spending the summer in Europe and handed him our pledge p a y m e n t s through September . . . when wham!"

1. The church needs the cash flow. The church that must wait for delinquent givers to "catch up" in the fall often must tap lines of credit. Whether done internally or externally, this nearly always results in extra costs.

2. Many people will not or cannot "catch up." Many persons who can

easily manage $20 per week suddenly find the prospect of making up an extra $100 balance impossible. Prepayment of a portion of this in the spring makes it more manageable.

3. The spring is an excellent time to ask for extra money. Psychology is on an upswing. Days are getting longer. Easter has just been celebrated. Vacations are being anticipated. People are *ready to give*.

4. A large unpaid balance carried over into fall often depresses the donor's motivation for increasing the pledge at campaign time (if that is also during the fall season). "How," the donor asks, "can I increase my pledge when I'm having trouble paying it now?" This is an entirely unnecessary question if you help the donor stay current.

While this technique is not for everyone, prepayment of a pledge has several advantages, some for the donor as well as the church. You might suggest prepayment in the following situations:

a. A lengthy planned absence such as going south for the winter or to the cottage for the summer which are both becoming more popular. The change in attendance patterns can have a devastating effect upon church cash flow, however. Many of your members could (and would) prepay their pledge if you asked and made it fun.

Why not have a special Sunday in the fall when you commission your "snow birds" to be your "Missionaries to Florida"? In addition to the fun of this recognition, many of these folks ought to be encouraged to prepay their pledge to help the church's cash flow. You also help the remaining congregation appreciate the important support of these persons.

b. To increase tax deductions. With the increase in the Standard Deduction, many persons discover they do not easily exceed the total necessary to secure a deduction for charitable contributions. Some thoughtful stewards prepay next year's pledge in December and secure enough to have a substantial charitable deduction. In the intervening year the Standard Deduction is taken. By exercising this strategy every other year, significantly increased deductions are possible.

c. To enable the church to avoid borrowing.—Because the deductibility of interest expenses is available to individuals, donors may prepay a pledge, operating or capital fund, to reduce the amount the congregation must borrow. Even if this requires borrowing the money for the prepayment, it is cheaper for the donor to borrow the money (and deduct the interest) than for the congregation to do so.

22. ELECTRONIC FUNDS TRANSFER

Fifty years ago almost no one gave money to the church by check; today it is the norm. Twenty years from now almost no one will use checks any more; electronic funds transfer will be the norm.

You can anticipate the future *and realize a substantial increase in income* by encouraging your people to use EFT today. The principles of EFT are simple.

1. The donor's pledge is in the form of an authorization for transfer of funds from his or her account to the church's account.

2. No other paper transactions (checks, deposit slips, etc.) are necessary.

3. The advantages to the donor are convenience, savings on check fees, postage, and envelopes.

4. The advantage to the church is improved cash flow and currency of pledge payment. According to a recent study, over 95% of donor pledges were fulfilled by those using EFT while a substantially lower fulfillment percentage resulted from conventional pledges.

In 1979 a Dallas Public TV station incorporated EFT into its fund drive with the following results.

- 13% of pledgers chose EFT.
- These 13% of donors contributed 29.4% of the dollars.
- The EFT pledgers actually gave an average of $76.53 compared to $27.097, the average for single payment pledges.

The advantages of EFT in fund-raising: By adopting a monthly giving plan which can be implemented efficiently and inexpensively, organizations can offer members and donors a convenient way to support the organization. With such a plan:

- Giving levels can be significantly increased and giving can continue regularly year after year.
- Donors who may previously have felt unable to make a significant contribution can do so.
- Since donors using EFT do not require repeated solicitation, solicita-

tion costs for EFT donors are reduced and efforts may be concentrated on non-donors.

- Billing and pledge reminder notices are not necessary to insure collection of pledged funds.
- Processing costs from EFT members or donors are significantly reduced since funds are transferred without manual handling of cash or checks.
- Payments are assured even in the event of postage tie-ups or strikes.
- Donors are relieved from continued solicitation and from the costs of writing checks and postage for mailing checks.
- Organizations are assured of regular monthly income, allowing more efficient management of funds.

How EFT works:

- An organization wishing to offer EFT services to its members or donors determines how to integrate the EFT method of giving into its present development plans.
- An authorization form is prepared.
- The authorization form is completed by the member or donor and returned to the organization.
- The organization provides the authorization form data to a NACHA member institution (a bank) or to a service institution for processing.
- The NACHA or Service Institution initiates deductions (debits) from the member or donor's checking account.
- Payments (credits) from the member or donor's checking account are put into the organization's account.
- The member or donor receives a record of the fund transfer on his or her bank statement.
- Summary reports and computer updates itemizing all EFT transactions made on behalf of the organization may be provided to the organization.

23. WHEN SHOULD WE CREATE THE BUDGET?

One of the most common strategic errors in carrying out the annual commitment campaign is the development of the budget for the coming year before the commitments are even received. This "Sell the Budget" style of campaign is ill-advised and nearly always self-defeating. What you had intended as helpful information in setting the congregation's sights higher, frequently results in quite the opposite reaction. Let's note some of the dynamics of this process.

First, you are making a declaration to the congregation that you have already made up your minds how much you are going to spend next year—irrespective of the response of the people. A donor prospect might conclude that his or her commitment is not very important—precisely the last thing you wish to suggest.

Next you have placed a ceiling on giving. Particularly if you note that this budget is a 5% increase over the preceding year's, don't be surprised if a 5% increase in giving is the top level of increase by an individual rather than the average. Your budget which you intended to be the floor has, in effect, become the ceiling.

You have placed yourself in the awkward position of having to defend your budget. This is a no-win situation. A detailed list of proposed expenditures is a laundry list of opportunities for finding fault. You are daring the recalcitrant to find something they don't like among your programs. Only the unimaginative will be unable to discover something they don't like. Even the presentation of a "Bare Bones" budget at a maintenance level results in this response. Here the donor will not likely find exotic program items against which to object but, conversely, will correctly observe that the church doesn't seem to be doing anything important. Thus the full-disclosure budget results in a "damned if you do, damned if you don't" situation. No matter what you present or don't present, you are displaying negative data.

Third, you are appealing to donors on precisely the wrong wave length. You have based your solicitation upon the congregation's need to spend rather than upon the donor's need to give. You have resorted to an entire campaign of raw fund-raising where you might have utilized your true resource—Christian stewardship.

We currently attend an unusual church quite unlike any with which I have ever been affiliated. In this wealthy congregation my wife and I know that our giving is almost incidental to the ministry of our church—there will be plenty of money whether we give through the church or not. This realization has had a salutary effect upon our appreciation of stewardship but also has helpfully reminded me of what you ought to remember always: Christians have a need to give quite apart from the church's need to spend. A budget-based campaign ignores this profundity.

Finally the budget-based campaign presumes that persons are motivated by numbers. Your experience should have convinced you by now that this is not the case. Persons are and always will be motivated by other persons.

Ask for commitments first. Create the budget later. Make quantities available for anyone who requests one, but be prepared for a surprise—few persons will even ask to see one.

PART THREE
Fund-Raising Strategies

1. SECOND CHANCE SUNDAY

Christianity is a "second chance" religion; that is what grace means. Each of us stands in need of the fresh start that God offers us. Finances are an excellent indicator of many other aspects of human life (see Luke 12:34). Many congregations have discovered how offering a "second chance" to donors will increase income to the church but also provide an exceptional spiritual opportunity for growth and renewal.

The principle of a successful Second Chance Sunday include the following:

1. A pledge that was made six months ago may no longer reflect accurately the donor's commitment or ability. Many persons are aware that they are in arrears on a pledge they fully intended to pay in full. This gives a splendid opportunity to catch up. Others will discover upon examination that last fall's pledge was unrealistically conservative.

2. Other persons have grown spiritually or in appreciation for the ministry of their church so that last fall's pledge no longer represents their commitment.

3. Opportunity to *designate* this second chance offering for a particular ministry rather than to a unified budget will be gratefully received by some persons. Often this technique alone will turn loose an extraordinary outpouring of giving.

4. Give yourself a minimum of two weeks during which to promote and educate. Use all available media. Stress that this will be a cash offering, not pledges. Also stress designated giving.

5. Give several options for designation. Perhaps you will want to choose the three most popular ministries you're currently doing or anticipating. Congregations typically choose something missional, something related to children and youth, and maybe something tangible such as building improvement or maintenance. Note that each of these options may be in the budget already. This second chance opportunity may well underwrite the entire yearly budget line item. This frees up these funds from offerings received during the other 51 weeks for more hard-to-sell ministries.

6. You may expect an offering somewhere between two and ten times the usual weekly offering. One small church with a usual weekly offering of $450-500 received over $5,500 in one day! A larger church with normal receipts of $2,600-2,800 received nearly $11,000!

2. PROHIBIT $1.00 BILLS

The dollar bill remains the basic denomination of special offerings. It is really a "token" gift: small enough not to hurt, large enough not to make noise. The trick in special offerings is to break out of the "token trap" and motivate the people to make a real gift.

"I would like to make this collection a kind of tribute to that great man, Abraham Lincoln. You will find a very good likeness of him on your five-dollar bills."

One method is to prohibit the use of dollar bills. Encourage your audience carefully to evaluate the cause and give in true proportion. Most donors could give a five dollar bill as easily as a one. Many will write a check for something between one and ten dollars. An occasional person may, in fact, find that one dollar actually describes his/her ability and interest. Ask these persons to write a check so you will know that they too have prayerfully considered the need and that their dollar is in true proportion.

You will find that the offering will be at least double the usual amount and, in many cases, substantially more than that.

This is one of those devices which can only be used sparingly but always works when used properly. If you have a particular need or special offering worth taking, it is probably worth a try at prohibiting $1.00 bills.

3. TITHING SUNDAY

Everybody knows what tithing is, but most persons' *experience* with tithing is vicarious, if at all. You will not make permanent tithers of your congregation easily, but the tithe can be used for an occasional "budget booster."

Challenge the membership to tithe on a specified Sunday. Give fair warning and perhaps even some aids for calculating the proper amount. Tell people they may tithe their gross or net income. (This helps to avoid the complaint that this tithe amount will announce one's level of income. Simply suggest that those who are embarrassed about their income level may tithe their gross, or more.)

You may expect an offering of at least double the usual amount and perhaps as large as 500%. Make certain that this event is part of a larger issue—a crucial need, tithing education, etc.

Tell what you received. This will give an exciting vision of the potential income your church could have if people would tithe regularly. One significant advantage of a tithing Sunday is that the burden falls most heavily on those who have been giving the smaller percentages. The faithful few who always tithe will not have to give more for this event (although some will).

Who knows, people may find that tithing feels good. Once they start, they may never quit.

Another alternative to a tithing Sunday is to challenge your members to give a day's pay for some special project. On a weekly scale this amounts to 20% of their earnings but may be a more effective technique for some donors to use in evaluating this challenge to their stewardship.

Some congregations have been successful in encouraging donors to consider a day's pay per month as their basic commitment to the church. This results in giving approximately 5% of income, a significant increase for many donors.

4. A CHRISTMAS WISH LIST

Christmas is a time for giving. Merchants know that. Advertisers know that. Your congregation knows that, too. Do you encourage them to make a special Christmas gift to the church? Why not make a "Wish List" of the things you "wish" the church would receive?

Think big. Make your list inclusive enough to allow for small gifts (perhaps from children) and substantial contributions. Offer local opportunities and world mission projects. Suggest tangible equipment needs and program possibilities.

Try something like this:

199X CHRISTMAS WISH LIST

- One piano—$2,200
- Electronic office typewriter—$1,100
- One earthquake-proof Third World house—$1,000
- Classroom table and 8 chairs—$700
- Sponsor for providing *Upper Room* devotional booklet to shut-ins— $300
- Four liturgical preaching stoles—$250
- Tuberculosis vaccine for 100 Haitian Children—$50
- Case of infant formula for emergency food program—$15.00
- Pew Bibles—$8.00 each
- Seed packets for Zambian farmers—$5.00 each
- Mittens for needy children—$2.00

5. THINGS TO DO WITH NICKELS (AND DIMES AND QUARTERS)

Most churches are long past the day when the morning offering included much loose change. Yet, properly raised, nickels, dimes, and quarters have the potential of adding up to a significant amount indeed. Use these strategies and watch the difference they make.

1. *Use Coin Collecting Devices*—At one time or another nearly everyone has used a coin folder. These little cardboard miracles show how dimes become dollars. The assumption of these devices is that giving is easier when broken down into the smallest possible unit. A dime a day should not be difficult for anyone, yet it translates into $3.00 in only a month, $4.00 during Lent. Why not use this technique for any special offering or project which requires more than $1.00 per person.

2. *"Two Cents Worth"*—We all like to get in our two cents worth. Think of some of the possibilities the 2 cents theme suggests. Two cents per person per meal becomes 24 cents a day for a family of four. That's $1.75 per week for missions, hunger, or any similar project. What would your mission budget be if your members all used this technique? In most cases the annual total would be double or triple the current level—all from *two cents worth!*

3. *Guilt Money*—To be effective the coin folder or canister must be in the right place. One place that has proven effective for some is, believe it or not, in *the refrigerator.* Thus, as backsliding dieters raid the icebox for that late evening snack they encounter the canister bearing the image of the starving child from Haiti. For some this cultural shock may be enough to put them off snacking at all. Others, however, have discovered that they are most willing to make that contribution to hunger ministries at this time. Somehow a quarter for hungry children doesn't seem like much for a person about to gobble a snack. Whether any guilt is assuaged or not, you'll raise more money if you invite people to put the folder/canister where it will do the most good.

4. *Tip the Waiter*—Isn't it interesting how the tip has increased over the years from 10 to 15% while the tithe is still 10%? Few indeed are the numbers willing to give 15% of their incomes to the church, but many could be challenged to give a "tip" of the cost of a meal to the cause of

hunger or some other ministry. Whether the meal is one eaten at home or in a restaurant is a matter of personal choice, but it provides an excellent context for a gift to world hunger.

10

"YOUR DIME ROLLED UNDER THE SEAT, MISTER."

6. SPONSORS

When should a budgeted item be in the budget? When its size or nature requires it to be shared by the entire congregation. When can an item safely be removed from the budget? Whenever an equally effective source of support can be found.

Just because the entire congregation may use or profit from a particular ministry doesn't imply that the entire congregation should pay for it. Many congregations have discovered that many church expenditures lend themselves well to individual sponsorship and, correspondingly, that many members are willing to sponsor a ministry or two.

The mechanics of sponsorship are simple: 1) tell which projects or programs you propose to finance through individual sponsorship; 2) tell how individuals may do so; 3) initiate a procedure for implementation of sponsorship and for recognition of the sponsor; 4) provide a simple procedure for these second-mile gifts to be remitted.

Ministries and programs where we've seen sponsorship used successfully include altar flowers, Sunday bulletins, newsletters, choir music, coffee hour refreshments, weekly bus expenses, insurance premiums, vacation Bible school materials, youth programs/events, camp fees, and family nights. Your imagination may well conceive other potential opportunities for sponsorship. The net result in every case is a substantial burden removed from the unified budget with an *increase* in enthusiasm from the sponsoring donor.

7. GIFTS OTHER THAN CASH

There are, in fact, two assets persons may give—cash and everything else. The congregation which insists on cash-only gifts will forego a substantial pool of potential gifts.

The reasons for giving non-cash assets will vary widely. In some cases securities, real estate, or other appreciated property will provide tax advantages that cash gifts can't match. Many persons are simply able to spare certain assets more easily than the cash equivalents. Others will want to preserve art works and similar assets by giving them to the local church.

Gifts in kind or services may have no tax consequences but will be attractive to the donor because it allows his/her personal resources to assist the church. People like to be appreciated for their unique contributions; it makes them special. For example, a country church I once served decided to paint the building, including the metal roof. The immediate dilemma was that no one wanted to do the highest parts of the roof. One man in the congregation, however, came forward and volunteered to do the "steeplejack" work. He proved to be totally fearless about heights and, although a previously inactive member, so enjoyed the praise and thanks he received that he began to attend regularly. His particular talent had been recognized and solicited. He had been glad to offer it. It was just the right thing to ask from him.

Your church has a great reservoir of talents and other non-cash assets which could be given. Do a little prospecting to discover what your members have to give and then ask them to give it.

An inner city church had a high percentage of low income members. It was difficult for these members to give cash, but they found great satisfaction in discovering assets they could give as expressions of their stewardship. A core of A.D.C. mothers discovered they could tithe their food stamps to provide food products for an emergency food ministry. Another low income woman lived in a housing complex. It was her delight to collect newspapers from her neighbors for all church paper drives. Yet another woman made it a point to solicit "leftovers" from her neighbors' garage sales from her church's free clothing program. She made certain that everyone holding a sale in her neighborhood knew that her church would be glad to receive what was left after the sale.

The only limit on non-cash gifts is your creativity in identifying what donors have to give and discovering how you can use it.

PART FOUR
Funds for Capital Projects

1. CONSTRUCTION FINANCING

Few projects have as great a potential for success or failure as the building of a new church or a substantial addition to an existing one. Financing a popular new church project may very well be the easiest financing project you'll ever undertake. Financing an unpopular church, however, is a devastating experience for any congregation. My assumption, however, is that you already have identified your construction project as a potentially popular one. Our task now, then, is to determine the most appropriate financing plan for your building project.

One of the substantial changes in the conventional wisdom today is the move away from mortgage as the rule of the day. Fifty years ago when buildings needed to be financed, the assumption was, and likely to be accurate, that the congregation had no funds of their own, and therefore a mortgage was in order. Mortgages were financed, with the building often as collateral and underwritten by a pledge drive, followed by subsequent pledge drives. For over fifty years this style of building financing has been effective and continues to be the norm.

However, today, the mortgage is still an option but no longer necessary. Many congregations are discovering that substantial resources are available within the congregation at any given time and that much more cash can be raised in a much shorter period of time than was ever thought possible. My current assumption is that 20% or more of the total cost of the project can be raised in any one day if a congregation really supports the building project. Indeed, if a congregation cannot raise 10% or more of the total building cost on one Sunday, serious thought ought to be given to whether in fact the project has wide and deep support.

The strategy that we use most typically to initiate such a program is to schedule a one-day in-gathering of significant proportions. Typically these days are called "Miracle Sundays" and in fact do stress high expectations from the congregation. The assumption is that this particular day will bring in 20% or more of the total building costs, in cash, not pledges, though the gifts may not be in cash but in the form of property, collectibles, assets of all kinds (see the separate entry describing Miracle Sundays).

One of the basic principles underlying the entire Miracle Sunday concept is to stress gifts coming from the capital of the donors. Persons do have money that is available now, since it is the donors within the congregation that will ultimately pay for the building construction, whether by paying off a mortgage from borrowed funds or by paying the cash. Currently it seems to be much more efficient to ask for the money now rather than to borrow and ask for the persons to give money to pay back the mortgage. In fact, even those younger members of the congregation who have substantially less capital and very limited available cash can be encouraged to borrow the money themselves and give the money to the church all in one lump. This reduces the need for the church to borrow, enables the donor to have, in fact, a double deduction. The gift itself is deductible whether it's paid in a lump or paid over a period of time, but then because they will also have interest costs on the money, donors can deduct the interest costs themselves where the congregation would not be able to deduct it (though this benefit may end in 1990).

Occasionally a congregation will try to finance its building by issuing notes to the membership—notes in varying multiples, varying maturity dates, and in some cases, demand notes. We are not trying to suggest that this is necessarily a good or a bad strategy. Notes ought to be issued only to accomplish two purposes: one, to achieve substantially less-than-market rates of interest and, second, with the understanding that some of the notes will not be redeemed. If, in fact, your assumption is that all of the note holders will ultimately ask for their money back, one should seriously question the validity and wisdom of offering notes in the first place. It is true, of course, that some donors are unable to make outright gifts to the church and that a lower rate of interest loan to the church might be the appropriate way for some persons to support the building program, whereas otherwise they might be unable to support it at all. These persons are a very small minority, however, and should not be the basis for a substantial commitment of the church's resources to this style of financing.

More likely, however, is the understanding that many of your persons who loan money to the church will ultimately never ask for it back. Some congregations discover that as many as half of their note holders forgive the note and never ask for a repayment. While this is a possibility in each congregation, you should not assume that that is the norm in yours. Conversely, you should not assume that every note will be repaid either. You won't know until you have some experience in this area.

One of the most successful note offerings involved a church that secured a semi-famous artist to produce a limited edition number of prints of a painting. On the back of the prints were printed the notes themselves. The prints were then framed, picture side out, and sold in the traditional note style. By the maturity date of the note, however, the artist had become sufficiently more famous that his prints were worth more than most of the notes and over 90% of them were never redeemed. Of course, I'm not suggesting that you try to develop such a relationship with an artist, but some circumstances do suggest the possibility that notes that are loaned are not necessarily notes that will have to be recalled.

One final concept to keep in mind whenever you're financing a new building: Once in every Christian's lifetime he/she ought to have the opportunity and the challenge to help build a church. In today's congregations many of our members have never seriously been a part of the excitement of a building program. They came into a church that was already there: they have lived and developed in a church that already existed. It met their needs and continues to meet their needs, but they have a priceless opportunity to build a church that will meet the needs of others yet to come.

2. PROSPECTING FOR BIGGER GIFTS

While visiting a farmer from his parish, a pastor decided to raise the subject of stewardship. "Brother Brown," the pastor inquired, "if a man had several 80-acre sections, would it be proper for the church to ask for one section?" Farmer Brown replied, "Why sure, pastor. That sounds fair to me."

"What about if a man has several tractors, might the church ask for one of those?"

"Of course."

"Well, what if a man had a herd of milk cows?"

"No, that isn't fair, Reverend. You *know* I've got milk cows!"

Perhaps the biggest hurdle in our efforts toward bigger gifts is that we do not know enough about our donors' ability to give, especially *what they have to give*. Dr. J. Oliver Buswell, when he was President of Wheaton College used to say, "Find out what a person owns and ask for one of them. If the person owns nine factories, ask for a factory." While I am not aware of anyone actually donating an entire factory to Wheaton College, you get the idea.

12

REV. TWEEDLE, D.D.

"One way or another Tweedle is going to raise the money for our church budget !"

Dr. Aryah Nesher of the United Jewish Appeal recommends checking out background information such as Dun & Bradstreet on major donors. In addition, you would do well to consult with friends and colleagues to discover more about *what* the donor owns—not necessarily how much.

The best strategy may well be to ask for clues directly from the donor. While many church members will be reluctant to volunteer information such as whether or not they own securities, real estate, collectibles, or life insurance, they may show an interest in receiving information about giving more effectively by utilizing those very assets. Offer free brochures for these asset-giving strategies and note who asks for them. A widow who requests material about giving stocks may be presumed to own some. Why not follow up with a request?

Items which are often overlooked as potential gifts but may be just the thing for a particular donor include U.S. savings bonds, antiques, art works, jewelry, life insurance policies, used cars, and various real estate properties. You might compile a file of information concerning the advantages of giving through these instruments. Encourage your donors to request information *before* making a charitable gift. The nature of their information requests will signal a good deal about donors' interests and assets.

Bob Sharpe tells of a congregation in which they explored the "A-B-C's of Giving" this way: Each Sunday the question was asked, "What could we give that starts with . . . . ?". For example, suggestions for "A" were *a*utomobiles, an *a*cre of crops, and *a*ntiques. "B" suggestions included *b*onds, *b*oats, and *b*argain sales. It's a great way to get people thinking about assets they might give.

3. FINDING BIG GIFTS

When a hospital sets out to raise $1 million for a new building it will likely use the "10-100-all the rest" principle. Briefly stated, this principle assumes that one third of the money will come from the top *ten* donors, the next third from the next *100* donors, and the last third from *all the rest*. What this means is that those top ten donors must average in excess of *$30,000 each*.

Do you receive gifts like that? If such large gifts are foreign to your congregation, it is time to ask "Why not?" There may be many reasons churches seldom receive large gifts while secular organizations do so routinely. It is not that our people are less prosperous (indeed the very persons who make the biggest gifts to all other charities are often members of local churches). It is certainly not that our cause is less important or attractive. What does make the difference?

Ashley Hale has correctly identified three prime reasons secular institutions receive large gifts.

1) The secular institutions have *big plans* for effectively utilizing big gifts. As the saying goes, "The squeaking wheel gets the grease." Major donors are accustomed to the world of major decisions, bold plans, and dramatic impact. Those organizations which can capture the imagination of persons of means must present a plan that is large enough for the donor to sense the excitement of it.

2) Successful institutions work on fund-raising the *whole year round*. It is not merely because secular organizations have employed fund-raising staff all year that they work at fund-raising all year. They understand (correctly!) that the task is that important. Large gifts are seldom generated because of a short-term campaign or emphasis. Big gifts come from an ongoing program of communication and development that works with donors while *they* make up their minds.

3) Big gifts go where somebody *asks* for big gifts. The first person to donate $1,000,000 to Robert Schuller's Crystal Cathedral was not a member. He was, in fact, a Lutheran. When Rev. Schuller asked him why a Lutheran would give a million dollars to the Crystal Cathedral, he replied, "The Lutherans *never asked* me for a million dollars!"

These three simple principles could be implemented by any church. With a little work, any congregation could formulate big plans—plans that excite and capture the imagination of donors. Any finance committee ought to give serious consideration to a year-long program of communication and stewardship development. The crucial dimension, however, is the last component—*asking* for the gift.

At this point allow me to anticipate some of your concerns and respond to them. I do not wish to heap guilt upon you or suggest that a lack of major gifts is an indicator of a major failure in your ministry. What it probably means more than anything else is that a tremendous potential awaits your congregation should you begin now to implement strategies which will result in big gifts for your church.

Many of you may be thinking that there is no potential for big gifts in your congregation because yours is not a wealthy congregation. Perhaps this is true (although there is likely to be a lot more wealth there than you think). However, your members need not be millionaires to be prospects for large gifts. Even a millionaire (and there are over 500,000 of them in the U.S. today!) will not give you a million dollars today. The largest gifts you are likely to receive will be *bequests*. Here almost any of your members may potentially leave the church a bequest in five or six figures. Most bequests in the $10,000 to $50,000 range come from persons who are not wealthy in the traditional sense at all.

Next, what *I* mean and what *you* mean when we say "large" gifts may vary substantially. I tend to think of any gift in five figures or more as a large gift. Perhaps $5,000 will qualify in your mind—that's fine. The point is that many of our folks could and would give much more if only we planned, acted, and asked for bigger gifts.

Finally there are many ways donors can begin *now* to provide a large gift some time in the future. Today's life insurance industry provides several ways in which many persons can allow money saved from income tax to do much of the financing for a substantial gift for their church in the future. For example, a 35-year-old professional woman in a high tax bracket can purchase a $100,000 life insurance policy with only five annual premium payments of $1,379. After the fifth payment, the policy is completely paid for and no premiums will be due again. If the woman should die, the church would receive $100,000. If she lives, the church may retain the policy or cash it in for the cash values ($26,098 at age 55; $62,485 at age 65). Because the church owns the policy, all premiums are tax-deductible, meaning the government may have paid for as much as *half the premium*.

Never assume there are no potential major donors in your church. Assume just the opposite and you will be right most of the time. Then you, too, will have found the fun of big gifts to meet the needs of your community.

4. THE A-B-C'S OF GIVING

A. *A*utomobiles, *a*cres of crops, *a*ntiques, *a*nnuities
B. *B*onds, *b*oats, *b*argain sales, *b*ooks
C. *C*ash, *c*ondos, *c*ollections, *c*ows, *c*rops
D. *D*iamonds
E. *E*state, *e*ndowment
F. Baptismal *f*ont, *f*arm
G. *G*ems, *g*old (jewelry, bullion, certificates)
H. *H*ouse, *h*ogs
I. *I*nvention (royalties), *i*ntangibles, *i*nterest (dividend assignment), *i*nventory, *i*nsurance, *I*RA
J. *J*ewelry
K. *K*ruggerand (gold)
L. *L*abor, *l*and
M. *M*oney, precious *m*etals, *m*otorcycle
N. *N*otes (treasury), *n*ecklaces, *n*uggets (gold)
O. *O*il (rights, royalties), *o*ptions (stock, etc.), *o*rgan
P. *P*ercentage of estate, *p*iano, *p*roperty (real)
Q. *Q*uarry, *q*uilt
R. *R*ings (jewelry), *r*eal estate, *r*efunds (tax), *r*oyalties
S. *S*tock, *s*ilver, *s*cholarship fund, *s*culpture
T. *T*estamentary *t*rust, *t*rusts
U. *U*sed car
V. *V*acation home, *v*iolin (antique), *v*olunteer labor
W. *W*ardrobe (deceased spouse), *w*atch (heirloom)
X. *X*erox machine (office equipment)
Y. *Y*acht
Z. *Z*ero coupon bonds

5. MIRACLE SUNDAY

What is happening when a congregation receives a Sunday offering that is equal to the combined offerings of the preceding 52 weeks? Clearly something miraculous is in our midst when such an event occurs. Yet this is happening in dozens of churches across the country. This phenomenon bears the generic name "Miracle Sunday."

Miracle Sundays may be utilized for a wide variety of causes but are most typically used for building and other capital projects. The results are dramatic, even miraculous, in proportions. Congregations report receipts of between 50% and 150% of the previous year's income. It is important to note that a gift is received, not a pledge. I say gift rather than cash because a considerable portion of the offering will be non-cash gifts. In fact, one measure of the effectiveness of a Miracle Sunday is the ratio of non-cash gifts to cash gifts.

We enthusiastically recommend Miracle Sunday because of three substantial benefits: First, this is an excellent method to test the level of support for a project. While many churches have been tentative in initiating a pledge campaign for a new building, a Miracle Sunday is a risk-free means of kicking off the building project. Though skeptics in the congregation are seldom impressed by pledges, nothing is quite as persuasive as cash/gifts. A pledge drive may succeed in securing an inflated level of commitments, pledges that will suffer a high rate of shrinkage. Miracle Sunday offerings, on the other hand, are firm and measurable. A congregation that can receive gifts equaling 20% of project costs or 50% of the previous year's income (whichever is less) has identified strong support for the project. Next, the "front loading" of a Miracle Sunday dramatically reduces the cost of capital by eliminating interest costs. Many churches have completely avoided the need to borrow funds by raising the total cost of the project with a Miracle Sunday. With the prevailing mortgage rates in double figures, total project costs can be triple the building's construction cost over a long-term amortization. It's good stewardship to avoid interest charges wherever possible.

Finally, we recommend Miracle Sundays because of the tremendous burst of enthusiasm and high morale that invariably occurs after a successful Miracle Sunday. It should be no surprise that churches behave differently when they are powerfully reminded that miracles still happen.

How much can be raised through a Miracle Sunday offering? We have found that most congregations can raise between 50% and 150% of the previous 52 weeks' income in a day. The primary determinants of this variance are the size of the project and the size of the congregation. Where the project is comparatively small, the results will likely be closer to the 50% level. Where the congregation is comparatively small, the results may exceed 100%. We have seen small congregations receive Miracle Sunday offerings in excess of 175% of the previous year's income. The smaller the congregation, the more dramatic the influence of individual large gifts.

Another rule of thumb we often use is establishing a Miracle Sunday goal of at least 20% of project cost. With all but the largest building projects, a successful offering ought to raise 20% or more of the total cost. Indeed, if much less than this is received, the congregation's leadership should hear an important message—either the congregation doesn't fully understand the project's benefits or, occasionally, the project is understood but rejected. Either way the results of a Miracle Sunday are "hard data" that can be interpreted. If the congregation is saying "No," you will be better off to hear the message at this juncture rather than after hiring expensive fund-raising counsel and conducting an exhaustive campaign, only to discover the same response.

HOW DOES A MIRACLE SUNDAY WORK?

Miracle Sundays can have many local variations, but all have three things in common:

1) *Clearly stated high expectations.* This cannot be presented as merely a "special offering." This is a time for miracles, not just a little more of the usual. It is not uncommon for a church to establish a goal of 100% of last year's budget or, with smaller projects, the total cost of the project. Imagine the excitement in a church when the leadership invites the membership to experience "the largest single offering in the history of our church"!

2) *Recognition by the congregation that there is a substantial stewardship value in avoiding debt* to whatever extent possible. Our "ace in the hole" for this concept is precisely the folks most important in ensuring the success of Miracle Sunday—our membership over age 50. Older members have a healthy respect for debt and readily agree that it is worth avoiding where possible.

3) *Gifts derived from the capital of your donors.* This event requires more than a little extra out of the paycheck. This concept is especially appropriate for Miracle Sundays because capital gifts match up well with a capital project such as a building addition. Ongoing ministries such as budgets and missions reasonably should come from an ongoing income source such as the income of your donors. Once-in-a-lifetime building projects, on the other hand, can be expected to receive extraordinary once-in-a-lifetime gifts from the capital of your donors. What this implies is that aging congregations which occasionally experience budget short-falls nevertheless can experience success on a Miracle Sunday which is more attuned to the capital-rich/income-poor circumstance of many of your members.

ORGANIZING FOR A SUCCESSFUL MIRACLE SUNDAY

Because many activities must be accomplished before your Miracle Sunday, we recommend allocating at least twelve weeks for this process. During this time momentum must be building, so care should be taken that the campaign not "peak" too soon. Miracle Sunday must be the absolute climax of the entire preparation period.

The leadership that you will require closely parallels that for an Every Member Commitment campaign, so refer to the separate entry describing campaign organization for EMC. Here we describe organization and oper-ation of the Miracle Sunday offering only. Whatever techniques you will use for presenting the "project" are beyond the scope of this section.

During the twelve weeks of the campaign you should make certain that good communication is continual. You can be sure of communication when many questions are surfacing. In fact, if you don't hear much from the membership, there is cause for alarm. Either your messages are being misunderstood or you are being rejected. A good Miracle Sunday is all but assured when you are receiving many questions about the project and Miracle Sunday itself.

Because the results of Miracle Sunday will be determined by your most active strata of membership, it is possible to take some significant liber-ties with the promotion process. Most significantly, it is usually not necessary to make home visits in promoting Miracle Sunday. Since your prospects are persons who are relatively active in the congregation, they can be expected to come to you.

The major components of the campaign are a direct mail program consisting of four mailings, two informational meetings, and a series of worship service announcements. Below is a brief timeline of the campaign and a summary of the content of each component.

TIMELINE TWELVE WEEK CAMPAIGN

Weeks 1-3   Leadership is recruited and campaign responsibilities established.

Week 4   Letter #1 announces Miracle Sunday and describes project. A project brochure is often helpful here. This letter should come from campaign chairperson or building committee chair.

Week 5 or 6 Meeting #1 presents building project plans with an emphasis on functions (benefits) rather than form of the project, what the building will do for us rather than what it will look like.

Week 7   Letter #2 gives update on Miracle Sunday and invites congregation to Meeting #2. Letter should come from most senior or respected member of the committee.

Week 8   Meeting #2 presents information on "How to Give to Make a Miracle Happen." Use some of the material in this chapter on capital campaigns (the A-B-C's of Giving, Finding the Right Stuff, Tax Efficiency, etc.). Because of the importance of this meeting, you may wish to schedule duplicate sessions.

Weeks 9 & 10 Letter #3 contains "testimonial" from respected lay leader. This is not so much a "sales" presentation as it is a statement of support for the project.

Week 11   Letter #4 is a pastoral letter from the clergyperson inviting everyone to attend Miracle Sunday and to pray for the success of this effort. A prayer vigil prior to Miracle Sunday is an appropriate option.

Week 12   Miracle Sunday! Include response cards for donors to use in indicating gifts to be given but not practical to bring to church that day (boats, automobiles, real estate, etc.).

Have a quick tabulation of receipts so you can announce the total before people go home. What excitement when you announce that you've exceeded your goal!

6. FINDING THE "RIGHT STUFF"

When we ask our members to give a major gift, help them identify the proper source from which to give it. While all gifts are about equal for the church to receive, they are by no means equal for the donor to give.

Finding the "Right Stuff" can be a most helpful exercise because it results in three likely outcomes:

1) Donors find the most appropriate source from which to make their gift. By "most appropriate" we mean the source from which a gift of the desired size can be given with the least "pain" or disruption of the donor's financial plan.

2) Donors are able to differentiate between what they *have* and what they *need*. This often identifies a surplus from which a satisfying gift can be made.

3) Donors frequently discover they can give *more* than they had anticipated—frequently at *less cost* than their expected gift might have meant to them.

How do we go about finding the "Right Stuff"? It is possible to begin the process by encouraging your members to ask themselves two questions:

1. What do I have? For this exercise you may wish to use something like "The A.B.C.'s of Giving" (p. 94) or some other means of helping donors take a quick inventory of what they own. You may wish to suggest a few common "gold mines," which many persons discover to be great sources of gifts. Ask about life insurance policies, securities, and collectibles. These are properties that donors frequently overlook but often find to be the best "source" of a satisfying gift.

2. What do I need? While you will never ask a donor to give the church something the donor needs, many persons will appreciate some help in sorting out the difference between "haves" and "needs." Life insurance is a common asset that becomes obsolete, that is no longer necessary for the purpose for which it was bought in the first place. Many donors are glad to give identified but unneeded assets to the church.

Another crucial distinction that often results in a major gift is that retirees may fail to recognize that the money in the bank they think they need is not really the issue. What many retirees really require is the *income* that money is producing. We have helped dozens of persons convert certificates of deposit to annuities after they discovered that these transactions resulted in thousands left to give the church. In many cases, this resulted when the donor found that converting to annuities allowed a current gift that otherwise might have been given through a will. The current gift was tax deductible to the donor, while the bequest would not have been.

In this process your most highly motivated donors will find sources from which they may give in larger amounts and with more satisfaction than they had imagined. In addition, when taxes are considered, the donor is often able to *give more at less cost*. This results in a happy donor, which is really the "right stuff" indeed.

PART FIVE
Promoting Your Financial Program

1. GIVE YOUR MAILINGS MORE IMPACT

Rocky Bridges, that colorful character from the baseball world, once said, "Here are three things people think they can do better than anybody else: build a fire, run a hotel, and manage a baseball team." My experience suggests that we might well add a fourth: *"Raise money by mail."*

Perhaps because mail is something we all receive and send, we feel more comfortable with it than with other media. This comfort, sadly, often leads us to a false optimism about our facility with mail-for-money. Here are some guidelines and strategies to assist you in giving your mailings the impact they deserve.

Guideline #1—If you are considering doing your solicitation entirely by mail, *don't!* Mail is too sophisticated an art form for most of us to use exclusively. It misses entirely a large segment of your congregation and significantly influences only a small segment. Your opportunity for feedback is severely limited. The almost inevitable result of a mail campaign is that those who are highly motivated to pledge will and those who are poorly motivated won't. Your mailings will have little influence on this pattern.

Guideline #2—Use mail as a component of a multifaceted campaign. Use mail for distribution of data of a factual nature.

- *Announce* the campaign.
- *Tell* that you are going to be visiting.
- *Invite* donors to bring pledges to worship on a particular Sunday.
- *Thank* those who participate.

Guideline #3—Don't use mail for motivational purposes. Mailings that are "homemade" seldom pack the punch necessary to do the job of motivating donors to do more. Conversely, professionally produced mailings often look so "slick" that there is a negative response from many donors. In a congregation, most real motivational work must be person-to-person, not person-to-paper.

Guideline #4—When you use mailings, differentiate them from your standard mail format. The very same inactive members who don't read your newsletter won't read your campaign literature if it looks like another newsletter. If you never enclose mailings in an envelope, send the campaign material in a #10 envelope. If you always mail in an envelope, consider sending campaign literature in mailable brochure format. *Make it distinctive.*

13

"I hate to see them close. They were always SO considerate about soft-pedaling any mention of money!"

Guideline #5—Use photos! Direct mailers have known for years that pictures tell the story better than the proverbial thousand words. This will probably mean that you will want to design special mailings rather than using your standard letterhead. The slightly increased cost will be more than worth it.

Guideline #6—If it looks and sounds like a business letter, scrap it and try again. The same style and tone that is appropriate when you communicate with strangers is out of place when you communicate with friends. The membership of your church ought to be your friends. Act like it. Don't worry about grammar or punctuation. Strive for communication. Keep it short, but consider using *two pages*. This will allow you lots of room for white space while still achieving the results of this discovery by direct mailers—*two pages* gets better results than one. Jerald Huntsinger, one of the gurus of direct response fund-raising, documents that 80% of the time a two-page letter outpulls a one-page letter and 65% of the time a four-page letter outpulls a two-page.

2. ADDRESS CORRECTION REQUESTED

If mail is worth sending out in the first place, it ought to be delivered. Yet in a mobile world where 20% of the households move every year, millions of pieces of bulk mail annually go undelivered. Why? Wrong address!

You don't need to lose track of your people. One of the best values the postal service offers is address correction. For a small fee the post office will provide you with the current address of anybody you mail to—but *you have to request it.*

Make certain that all your bulk mail is marked "Address Correction Requested." It's a small investment to keep track of your members. It pays dividends over and over again.

3. EIGHT KEYS TO THE KINGDOM— SOLICITATION STRATEGIES

Here's a quick quiz of your stewardship strategy savvy. Below are the eight most commonly used methods of receiving financial commitments in the church today. Rank them 1 to 8 in the order of their effectiveness.

_____ A. Personally written letters
_____ B. General mail appeal
_____ C. Loyalty Sunday
_____ D. Congregational dinner
_____ E. Small group meeting
_____ F. Telephone canvass
_____ G. Personal visitation
_____ H. Saddlebag method

A widely accepted ranking of effectiveness is found below, but let's look at each of these strategies in order of popularity. Note that popularity has little to do with effectiveness and much to do with simplicity.

General mail appeal—Probably the most popular of any campaign except possibly for "no campaign at all." This strategy is easy to do with most of the work performed by the church staff. The success of these campaigns is based upon the faithful giving of persons who would have responded to *any* campaign.

Loyalty Sunday—Members bring commitments to a designated worship service. This is an excellent way to promote commitment rather than merely fund-raising. Its major weakness lies in the obvious limitation of reaching only those who participate in that particular worship experience.

Saddlebag method—See separate entry (p.15) for pros and cons. This is primarily a *collection* procedure to receive commitments already made by the donor. There is little opportunity for influence.

Small group meeting—Has a substantial advantage over home visitation in that the message may be delivered more efficiently to a group rather than repetitively to individuals. The flip side of this advantage is that the group setting frequently limits true dialogue. This strategy is most effective for building campaigns where a major part of the visit is interpreting the project.

Congregational dinner—Very similar to Loyalty Sunday except the energies are directed toward encouraging participation at the dinner rather than a worship experience. At the dinner the presenters interpret the ministry and program of the church. This method often fails because of its limited "reach" and the fact that the congregation's program is seldom a true motivator of giving.

Telephone canvass—A growing phenomenon that is becoming more popular. As with the "saddlebag method," every family is touched with a human contact, in this case via phone. With a carefully written "script" callers can accomplish a lot through this medium. It is best to utilize a "survey" format where more information is requested than "How much will you give?"

Personally written letters—Campaign leaders personalize mailings to the membership, often handwriting the solicitation materials. The goal is to appear "user-friendly." The reality, however, is a frequent perception that this was an excuse not to visit or phone.

Personal visitation—In a world characterized as "high tech," people have a longing for "high touch" contacts with another person. This method is without question the most difficult but, without much doubt, the most effective method of all.

It should be remembered that there is no "one size fits all" financial campaign strategy. With experience and a little adaptation, you may find the most effective style of reaching your members with your message, your way.

Many experienced stewardship leaders would rank the eight methods
1) G   2) F   3) H   4) C   5) D   6) E   7) A   8) B.

PART SIX

Planned Giving Strategies
For Today and Tomorrow

1. PLANNED GIVING

Of all the possible sources of financial growth, I am convinced that planned giving offers the largest growth potential.

1. Planned giving is where the money is. Just as Willie Sutton claimed he robbed banks because that was where the people kept the money, planned giving affords access to the largest pool of potential gifts. While the weekly offering will nearly always be a portion of the last two weeks' income, planned gifts come from the reservoir of resources accumulated during a lifetime.

Bequests alone now account for over $3.5 billion in charitable gifts each year. Moreover, amounts of planned gifts are growing much more rapidly than current gifts. Giving from all sources increased 12.3% over 1980 during 1981, but bequests grew 21.7%! In 1982 bequests increased 27% more. The trend continues, and the church must respond to it.

2. As our membership ages, the potential for planned giving increases. Today churches report that their active membership is increasingly characterized as older. In many (if not most) churches, gray heads predominate.

While our members become older, they struggle with the reality or the prospect of decreased income at retirement. While many faithful members reallocate funds so that their pledges are continued into retirement, many are unable to increase their giving or to respond to special, extra-budget opportunities. This is where planned giving becomes more than a funding source; it becomes a funding *service.*

The church that helps its members discover their planned giving potential provides an important service to seniors who otherwise would miss the joy of participating in special mission, building, or other projects.

Many forecasters and leaders debate the wisdom of the demographic trends which suggest that our active church membership is increasingly elderly and female. For our purposes, however, let it be said that this demographic shift is precisely in the direction of increased planned giving potential. The ideal planned giving prospect, say the experts, is a retired widow. If this reflects our current constituency, let us at least phrase our stewardship appeals in terms which are most useful to the elderly.

3. Finally, planned giving is the easiest kind of giving to "sell." The nature of planned gifts, particularly deferred gifts, is that they are "painless." While every time the offering plate is passed our people must give us money they would otherwise have spent on themselves, planned giving instruments often offer the intriguing possibility of giving from funds we aren't using or couldn't use anyway. We are offering persons a splendid opportunity to exchange "that which they cannot keep for that which they can never lose."

The phenomenon of credit purchases, while somewhat different, is an interesting parallel. Increasingly, Americans are buying on credit. There may be many reasons why this phenomenon continues, but certainly one major factor is the psychological impact of receiving the goods immediately while deferring payment. The satisfaction of the purchase is immediate, while the "pain" of paying for it comes much later. Planned gifts present an even better opportunity for this phenomenon. Because many planned giving instruments are funded from the donor's estate only after death, the satisfaction of the gift is given immediately and lasts for life, while the cost of the gift is never felt at all. This is no sleight of hand; it is an important stewardship opportunity to offer our members.

Some of the following planned giving instruments may seem complex and intimidating. This is not really the case, however. These are really vehicles that most any motivated Christian steward could utilize. We have intentionally avoided the more complex planned giving devices or those applicable only to the very wealthy. What follows are instruments which call our members to reflect upon their giftedness and respond intentionally rather than reflexively. It is this intentional nature of planned gifts that makes them marvelous expressions of Christian stewardship and, only coincidentally, the source of great giving potential.

2. WILLS

We begin with wills because of two fundamental advantages wills have over other planned giving devices.

1. Everybody knows what a will is. Unlike trusts, life estate contracts, and many other instruments, we may assume that our people already know what a will is. Many of your members do not understand what a will can *do,* but they at least know what a will *is.*

2. Everyone needs a will. You may find that some folks are convinced that they *don't* need a will. Joint ownership, small estates, and lack of heirs are commonly cited reasons some persons feel they don't need a will. Yet it is a fact that few persons are completely happy with the way their property will be distributed if they die without a will. Even if an unusual person should wish to allocate property completely consistent with the law of descent and distribution of property in his/her state, the church can raise one indisputable claim. No bequest can be made without a will.

If, as I firmly believe, one's intentional Christian stewardship is incomplete without a bequest in one's estate plan, a will is a necessity to make it happen.

Begin your planned giving emphasis with education about wills. People know what you're talking about, but most folks don't have one yet.

Surveys consistently report what probate courts substantiate—most people don't have wills. While over $120 million is piling up in probate courts each week from intestate estates, less than half the population has a will. According to data gathered by the North American Interchurch Study, only 15% of laity in the U.S. have a will in which they have included a bequest for the local church. The most commonly cited reason for not doing so, as incredible as it may seem, is, "It never occurred to me." Clearly we have a huge recource for growth.

Appendix A includes some simple steps for getting your wills emphasis off the ground. Start with basic information about what a will can do, move into a discussion of what bequests can do for your church, and help persons know the satisfaction of a Christian estate plan.

3. HAVE A WILLS CLINIC

Since "a lot of what people 'know' about wills isn't really so," you will need to do some education. A Wills Clinic is a simple programmatic means to get the word to the right people in the most practical way.

Here are the basic steps to follow for an outstanding Wills Clinic.

PREPARATION

1. Decide who should come. Perhaps you will schedule the clinic as a program for an already existing group—senior citizens, women's group, couples club, whatever. Otherwise you'll need to target a group. In general, older folks and young married couples have differing concerns which suggest separate clinics for each group.

2. Set the date and begin the promotion.

3. Invite the panel. This is a topic for which you can usually get the best "experts" in town to come *absolutely free.* Lawyers, C.P.A.'s, life underwriters, development officers, and denominational foundation directors all have something to offer your people, and all will come without charge. Most will be pleased to be asked. At the absolute minimum, your panel should include an attorney and someone else trained in planned giving. Your denomination will probably have a staff person to offer.

PROGRAM

1. Welcome the audience. Introduce the panel. Give a brief statement of the purpose of the meeting. For instance, "We are here this evening to gain information about the benefits of making a will. We'll learn a bit about legal aspects, how to give through a will, and how to secure our estate plan with a will."

2. Have a brief presentation which should show why wills are important. A good audiovisual presentation is usually best. Keep it short; thirty minutes is about maximum.

3. Let the panel respond. Give panel members 2-5 minutes each to make any observations they wish.

4. Take a break. Many persons will not ask important questions in front of a group. A break for coffee will enable these persons to approach the "experts" and ask questions in private.

5. Reconvene for questions from the audience.

6. Make certain that the matter of bequests is mentioned. This should not be the major emphasis of the clinic but should not be forgotten either.

7. Adjourn. Let the pastor or host give a concluding prayer and wrap up the evening in 90 minutes or so.

FOLLOW-UP

Keep track of persons who have attended wills clinics. You may wish to communicate with these folks occasionally about bequests and other estate planning topics. These persons are your primary market for bequests. Use them.

Tell about wills, over and over again.

Fill in the corners of newsletters and bulletins with wills information. A "teaser" message could be the impetus someone may need to make that first contact. Even a single line reminder that the church wants bequests could be the difference for somebody.

Here are some samples that you may wish to duplicate.

WHAT ARE THE
ADVANTAGES OF
INCLUDING THE
CHURCH IN MY WILL?

Date Used

/ /

WHAT ARE THE ADVANTAGES OF INCLUDING THE CHURCH IN MY WILL?

Spiritually, everything. By remembering the church, you acknowledge your debt to God and express your continued stewardship by furthering God's work even after your death. Charitable giving has become an accepted part of our society for many reasons. Aside from humanitarian, moral and religious aspects, tax benefits have assumed increasing importance. The government actually encourages people to leave money and property to religious, charitable, and educational institutions by exempting them from inheritance taxes. Any property you leave your church or institution is tax exempt.

HOW LONG IS A WILL GOOD?

HOW LONG IS A WILL
GOOD?

Date Used

/   /

A will is valid until it is changed or revoked. However, marriage of the testator after a will has been written may substantially alter the effect of the will. A change in other circumstances, such as tax laws, marriages, births or deaths in a family, divorces, or even a substantial change in the nature or amount of a person's property holdings may make a change in a will desirable, to conform to a testator's wishes under the new conditions.

DOES YOUR STEWARDSHIP END WITH DEATH?

DOES YOUR
STEWARDSHIP END
WITH DEATH?

Date Used

/   /

Christians are God's stewards. Everything we possess is the gift of God. We are stewards of all we own and we are stewards of what we shall leave in this world when we depart this life. Only we have the privilege and responsibility to decide what shall be done with our possessions here and hereafter. Through a will, earnest church members can assure themselves that their Christian stewardship will not end with their death. Through wills people can not only deepen their own spiritual life, but they can expand service of the church far beyond their own lifetime. They can help the great humanitarian work of the church in their own community and throughout the world.

YOUR WILL, WHY DO YOU NEED LEGAL ADVICE?

YOUR WILL, WHY DO
YOU NEED LEGAL
ADVICE?

Date Used

/   /

Good intentions are not enough for drawing a valid will. Your intentions must be stated in accordance with the laws of your state and expressed in language that cannot be misinterpreted. Only a competent attorney can help you draw your will so that it can carry out your wishes exactly. Remember, you will not be present to clarify any misunderstandings. A valid will must clearly express your intention, using appropriate language to provide for the transfer of property interests under the existing laws.

WHEN YOU INCLUDE
THE CHURCH IN YOUR
WILL

Date Used

/ /

WHEN YOU INCLUDE THE CHURCH IN YOUR WILL

A bequest in your will may be directed to support the general cause of the *(here insert the legal name of your local church)* or to one or more specific purposes. For example you may wish to make a bequest in your will to provide for capital improvements or a scholarship fund or some specific church equipment. The *Discipline* of The United Methodist Church provides that bequests are received by the church trustees under the direction of the Charge Conference. Your pastor can assist you in the selection of specific bequests.

BEFORE YOU MAKE
YOUR WILL

Date Used

/ /

BEFORE YOU MAKE YOUR WILL

1. Make a list of all your assets—money, property, valuables—and the exact name in which title is held.
2. Prepare a list of loved ones and friends whom you wish to remember in your will.
3. Write down the name of your church and/or any church causes or institutions to which you wish to make bequests.
4. Write out exactly how you wish your assets to be distributed.
5. Discuss with your pastor ways by which you can make your "will power" help in the work of Christ and the church.
6. Make an appointment to see your attorney; show him/her your memorandum, and ask him/her to draw a will for you in accordance with your wishes.

The cost of preparing a will is very nominal. Your attorney can advise you about appointing an executor, taxes to be paid or saved, and other helpful suggestions.

REVIEW YOUR WILL

Date Used

/ /

REVIEW YOUR WILL

A will expresses the manner in which a person wishes his or her estate to be distributed in the event of his or her death. Since situations and circumstances change, it should be kept up-to-date. Some of the events which may affect your will are: births, deaths or disability, marriages and divorces of beneficiaries or executor, changes in manner of holding property, change of residence, changes in laws, change in economic conditions, and many others. Since a will should be prepared by your attorney, it should be also kept up-to-date through frequent interviews with him or her.

STEWARDSHIP
THROUGH A WILL

Date Used

/ /

STEWARDSHIP THROUGH A WILL

Many voices in our day emphasize the wisdom of making a will. These add strength to our conviction that the church renders a service when it encourages its members to make wills. A will enables one to continue special interests after death; perpetuates one's influence and personality for generations; guarantees a safekeeping of Christian enterprises; and influences lives which follow. It is a confession of the stewardship of God's gifts which provides for the continuing support of the influence and ministry of Christ and God's kingdom. A will is an investment in eternity and immortality.

A WILL—THE
"MOMENT OF TRUTH"

Date Used

/ /

A WILL—THE "MOMENT OF TRUTH"

You face the "moment of truth" when you become actively concerned about your will. Memorable events and interests in your life may flash before you as you recall those people and situations most meaningful to you. Your family and loved ones and your own church which nurtured you during your life will be of primary concern. By making a will, a person plans the disposition of the fruits of an entire life's work, the welfare and future of loved ones, and the strengthening of the causes and institutions which have meant most in one's life.

ABOUT THOSE "HANDY
PRINTED FORMS"

Date Used

/ /

ABOUT THOSE "HANDY PRINTED FORMS"

Drawing a will is not a "do-it-yourself" proposition. Only a "FORMS" lawyer has the special education and experience to draft a will. Printed will forms where one simply "fills in the blanks" and saves a lawyer's fee can be disastrous. Ready-made wills necessarily must be designed for a hypothetical average person. And in real life, nobody is "average" in assets and circumstances, or in hopes and plans for the future welfare of dependents and loved ones. Certainly the causes and institutions to which each individual is devoted are as different as night and day. To be valid, your will must declare your own personal intentions as to the distribution of your possessions. A shortcut that purports to "save" lawyer's fees could prove the world's worst bargain for your heirs and beneficiaries—and your church.

4. SHOW YOU KNOW WHAT TO DO WITH BEQUESTS

The church treasurer paused and squinted as he attempted to remember. "How many bequests have we received? Well, as far as I can remember, in the last 35 years, one—I guess." Incredible! Only one bequest in 35 years—what's going on here?

That church, whether it realized it or not, was sending out the message—"Please don't remember us with bequests. We really don't know what we would do with them." No policy for bequests is a policy for *no bequests*.

Before you begin to solicit bequests from your membership, show that you know what to do with the money when you receive it. Establish policies which give persons reasons to want to give rather than reasons not to.

Anticipate the concerns of your people. Typical questions are:

1. If I make a bequest, will the church spend the money frivolously?
2. Will the church invest the money? How?
3. If I make a substantial bequest, will it undermine the level of stewardship for future generations?
4. What types of projects could be funded by bequests?
5. Who will be responsible for administering bequests, endowment funds, and endowment expenditures?

Sound policies which put to rest unnecessary apprehensions will encourage your members' natural desire to give through bequests. Money goes where it is needed. Charitable giving goes where it seems to do the most good. Give people reasons to give instead of excuses for not giving.

Appendix D includes some sample policy statements concerning endowment, investment, and use of funds.

5. PROVIDE FOR A LOVED ONE AND THE CHURCH: TESTAMENTARY TRUSTS AND GIFT ANNUITIES

It is possible to use a will to provide support for a loved one and the church with the same instrument. A donor's will can establish a testamentary trust or gift annuity. In each case, a beneficiary named by the donor will receive an income for life with the remainder of the asset going to the church when the beneficiary dies.

This is an important consideration for many donors who want to provide for a spouse or friend, while also providing a gift for the church. This device is especially attractive to donors in this era of remarriage in widowhood. Without taking any assets away from a beloved spouse, the donor can insure that a gift will be made to a church or charity irrespective of any subsequent marriage or asset distribution.

Such a testamentary trust or gift annuity becomes, in essence, a gift that gives twice.

Here's how it might work.

The donor's will provides that a trust or gift annuity be established to provide income for the loved one for life. This can be a fixed amount, such as an annuity, or a floating amount based upon a percentage of the assets, as in a trust. Upon the death of the income beneficiary, the remaining amount will go to the church. This charitable "remainder" gift results in a tax deduction for the donor's estate. Note: If current tax deductions are desired, the trust or gift annuity must be established other than through the donor's will. See the entry on life-income gifts.

6. GIVE GOD A HOUSE: LIFE ESTATE CONTRACTS

Many persons within your church have long harbored a desire to make a substantial gift to the church. For most of them, however, the economic pressures of life seem to render these dreams impossible. There simply is not enough money to spare. There is, however, an important asset that could be the answer for many of your members—their house.

A *Life Estate Contract* is a device that often enables persons with limited resources but high giving interest to realize the satisfaction of a major gift without economic sacrifice. The provisions of a life estate contract generally include the following:

1. Title to donor's home (or family farm) is given to the church or charitable institution.
2. Donor retains all rights to the property for life. This includes the right to live in the house, make any decorating changes desired, and receive any income generated by the property. Donor also retains all the attendant responsibilities—taxes, upkeep, etc.
3. Donor receives an immediate tax deduction for the present value of the remainder interest of the property. In many cases, this means the donor will pay no income taxes for as many as five years!
4. Upon the donor's death the property passes to the church without restriction.

This instrument is not for everyone but provides a marvelous opportunity for some persons to make a satisfying gift. Because possession of the assets does not change until after death, this is the closest thing to "giving your property and still having it." This is an especially good giving instrument for land-rich/cash-poor donors.

Why not contact your church's neighbors? Even if they are not members of your congregation, many of them have had a relationship with the church for years. Their property might be just what the church needs for expansion, parking, or some other good purpose. Occasionally the tax advantages of exchanging a house which they can't keep anyway, for tax-free income for five years will be sufficient motivation to make such a gift.

Do your people know about Life Estate Contracts? Why not tell them? You never know when someone will decide to give God a house.

Appendix C shows a sample Life Estate Contract Agreement.

7. TRUSTS: AN INTRODUCTION

Charitable trusts are giving instruments which will usually require expert advice but will also provide unique advantages to both donor and beneficiary. Some of the advantages possible through trusts are:

1. Opportunity to make a gift of an asset while retaining income from it for life (often for the life of a spouse as well).

2. Opportunity to receive a tax deduction now on gifts that would otherwise pass only after death.

3. Opportunity to fund one's current giving with a gift which will generate income forever.

4. Opportunity to give to one's church while still providing for a relative or other loved one.

5. Opportunity to give to more than one charity through one instrument.

6. Opportunity to avoid probate for reasons of convenience, timing, or privacy.

7. Opportunity to transfer investment responsibilities to a charitable organization. Many persons (especially widows) prefer not to have responsibility for investing assets. The Charitable Remainder Trust enables them to receive a good income without the worry or work of investment.

There are myriad other potential advantages which individual donors may discover through the use of charitable trusts. A qualified estate planner will be able to point them out for you.

THE LANGUAGE OF TRUSTS

Trusts will seem much less intimidating if you learn a few key terms and phrases. Here are the basic components of trust terminology and simple descriptions of each.

- *Donor*—(sometimes called the *creator, settlor,* or *trustor)* the one who creates the trust, the person giving the property included as trust assets
- *Trustee*—the person or institution holding title on behalf of someone else, the person or institution managing the trust for someone else's benefit
- *Testamentary trust*—a trust arrangement created through a will
- *Inter Vivos Trust*—literally a trust "between living beings," a trust created and activated during the donor's lifetime
- *Beneficiary*—someone who benefits from a trust, usually one who receives income from a trust

TYPES OF TRUSTS

There are three basic forms of charitable trusts.

1. *Charitable Remainder Unitrusts* give the beneficiary a fixed percentage (5% or more) of the assets annually. The trustee establishes the value of the assets annually and the stated percentage of that amount is paid. A tax deduction is received on a portion of the initial trust assets depending upon age and gender of the donor. For example, a male age 55 creates a 6% unitrust of $10,000. He receives charitable tax deduction of $3,822 plus income for life. Upon the death of the donor the charity receives all the remainder of the trust assets.

(Note: A *Charitable Remainder Annuity Trust* is similar to the Charitable Remainder Unitrust except that the income to the beneficiary is a fixed dollar amount which will not vary according to the value of trust assets.)

2. *Pooled Income Funds*—A charity creates a fund into which a number of donors contribute funds. Each donor receives a pro rata share of the earnings of the fund for life (and for the life of another beneficiary also, if desired). Because these funds are distributing income on a pro rata basis rather than according to donor age, they often are able to pay a higher rate of interest. The charitable tax deduction, however, is determined by donor age. Upon death of the beneficiaries, the funds become property of the charity.

3. *Gift Annuities* are not technically trusts. They are a combination of gift and purchase of an annuity. The donor or beneficiary receives a

guaranteed amount for life. This dollar amount is determined by the Committee of Gift Annuities' actuarial tables. Two significant tax consequences accrue to the donor: an immediate deduction of a portion of the gift amount (determined by age) and tax-free income for life because up to ⅔ of the annuity is considered returned principal and not taxed.

(Note: Both Pooled Income Funds and Gift Annuities usually require state licensing before your organization may issue either instrument. Here is a good place to use your denominational foundation.)

8. HAVE AN ESTATE PLANNING WORKSHOP

After you have promoted wills for a period of time, the next step is to educate the congregation about other estate planning strategies. One of the best ways to do this is to schedule an Estate Planning Workshop.

Here are the basic steps to follow for an outstanding Estate Planning Workshop.

PREPARATION

1. Unlike a Wills Clinic, a good estate Planning Workshop should be targeted to a much more limited audience. Since this is the next step beyond wills education, you should consider persons who have participated in Wills Clinics or who are otherwise known to have a will. Decide if you need to address a wide variety of estate planning principles or if there are specific concerns people are asking about.

2. Set the date and begin promotion.

3. Make the invitations. If you anticipate a large group, you may wish to segment your audience with separate workshops for younger couples, older couples, and singles.

4. Invite a good panel. Lawyers, C.P.A.'s, life underwriters, trust officers, and denominational planned giving officers would be good resources for your panel. Because some of the strategies to be explored are complex, your lawyer should practice estate planning as a specialty.

PROGRAM

1. Welcome the audience. Introduce the panel. Give a brief statement of purpose for the meeting. You might say something like, "We are here this evening to learn more about estate planning. We'll learn some strategies for making dreams into plans, making plans into realities, and for securing all this with a carefully crafted program."

2. Have a quick review of the importance of wills. Perhaps the attorney could summarize the critical issues in ten minutes or so.

3. Introduce a related estate planning issue. Perhaps a good film or other audiovisual resource would be appropriate.

4. Panel discussion. Allow each professional to make whatever observations seem most relevant from his/her particular perspective.

5. Take a break. It is a good idea to provide some opportunity such as a coffee break for persons to approach the panel members with personal questions.

6. Take questions from the audience. The convenor might take the question, repeat it to be certain it is understood by both audience and panel, then direct it to the appropriate panelist.

7. Make certain that someone discussed ways charitable giving can be a part of good estate planning.

8. Adjourn. Let the pastor or host thank the panel, give a concluding prayer, and send the people home, enriched for having come.

FOLLOW-UP

Persons who have attended Estate Planning Workshops are excellent prospective donors. Keep track of who has attended. Communicate with them occasionally to discover if they need more information or what they are doing with current information. Some of those folks may be appropriate to serve on a Wills, Memorials, and Estate Planning Committee.

9. THE ASSET EVERYONE HAS: TOTTEN TRUSTS

Although the form continues to change, the asset everybody owns is still a bank savings account. These accounts will automatically be included in a donor's estate for distribution by will or law unless a special arrangement transfers the assets *by contract.*

An excellent giving device for many donors is the establishment of a "Totten Trust." This is, in reality, a bank account owned by one person and "payable on death" to another. In this day and age, when people tend to have several different investment vehicles, the *Totten Trust* is an easy way to make a gift at death without a will, a codicil to an existing will, or any significant expense.

WIZARD OF ID 14

Here's how it works. The donor simply establishes the account in this way: "John Doe in trust for First Church." This means that John Doe owns the account and may make any deposits or withdrawals he wishes. When he dies, the account becomes the property of First Church. First Church has no rights to the account until Mr. Doe's death.

In addition to savings accounts, savings certificates (C.D.'s), and most mutual funds may be established as Totten Trusts.

10. THE I.R.A. AND PENSION PLAN GIVING

An increasingly large portion of our people's total assets are in the form of various pension plans. The newest and fastest growing area is Individual Retirement accounts (I.R.A.'s). The Economic Recovery Tax Act of 1981 opened the door for millions of persons to establish I.R.A.'s. What's more—they're doing it.

Forbes Magazine forecasts that by 1992 no less than *$3 trillion* will be in pension plan accounts— with I.R.A.'s an important part. By law, none of this large pool of resources can go to churches *unless the donor authorizes* it.

Your church could be the final beneficiary of I.R.A.'s. Unlike many employer-paid plans, I.R.A.'s have cash values which must be paid out. The money is paid to the owner/beneficiary, to the estate upon the owner's death, *or to a designated final beneficiary.*

Unless you call this to the attention of your membership, most folks won't know that this can be done. And unless you actively solicit gifts from I.R.A.'s, you will be overlooking a huge source of potential gifts.

PENSION PLAN GIVING

Many pension plans offer givers a marvelous opportunity to make planned gifts at no cost to them. Because modern plans are vested and annuitized for a guaranteed minimum period (5 years certain, 10 years certain, etc.), donors can name the church to be the residual beneficiary. This means that the donor loses no pension benefits; only the balance not yet paid at death will be transferred to the church.

Pension funds are big. For many persons with few liquid resources, pension plan gifts represent the largest potential giving device. Help donors see how they can transfer some of these funds at absolutely no cost to them. You will be helping the donor and also tapping a huge source of potential funds.

(See also the section above highlighting I.R.A.'s.)

11. GIVE BY CONTRACT

In addition to wills and trusts, contracts provide an excellent vehicle for many persons to make planned gifts. Most persons already have made provision for transferring property by contract even if they don't know it. Joint ownership is a commonly used form of contract transfer as are life insurance and pension plans.

Churches can be the beneficiaries of many contract gifts. In this section we will suggest some new income sources for your church that are real possibilities for many of your donors—all by contract.

Contract giving is attractive to many people for the following reasons:

1. They are simple to establish. Most of these giving instruments require no professional legal advice or extra cost.

2. They often use assets with which persons are familiar (life insurance, pension funds, bank accounts) but offer new possibilities as charitable gifts.

3. Most contracts are easy to change or abolish. This provides a substantial dose of peace of mind.

4. They allow property to pass immediately at death (or some other stated time) without the necessity of probate.

Tell your congregation about giving by contract. Show them how. A few of the most commonly used contract-giving opportunities follow.

12. TEN WAYS TO USE LIFE INSURANCE FOR PLANNED GIVING

Life insurance has been around for only 200 years or so but now represents a $1½ *trillion* business. The average family owns more than $25,000 in life insurance, yet little of this money ever finds its way into the church. This pool suggests a tremendous potential for charitable gifts.

Life insurance has great appeal for many donors because it uses a resource with which they are familiar and requires no special legal consultation or fees. Life insurance provides a simple, convenient instrument with which donors can give larger and more satisfying amounts than would otherwise be possible. Insurance provides options through which gifts may be made immediate, later, and in combination.

Some of these strategies require new policies, but most utilize existing policies. Many churches are discovering much interest in learning about giving through life insurance. Why not highlight one or two of these ten strategies each week for a month or so? Somebody may even suggest number eleven.

INSURE A PLEDGE

Mr. Brown was a saint. The grand old man had been a substantial giver to all the programs of East Cupcake Church for years. It surprised no one when his ten-year pledge for the new educational building was the largest of all. But Mr. Brown died in the second year of the campaign, leaving an unpaid balance of more than $8,000 of his pledge. What a wonderful surprise it was when Steve Smith, Mr. Brown's insurance agent, phoned with the good news that Mr. Brown had thoughtfully insured his pledge with a decreasing term policy payable to East Cupcake Church! A check for $8,480 was in the mail.

Many of your best givers would be glad to pay the little extra to insure their pledge. It may be possible to have an agent within the congregation sell the policy and donate the commission. In any case, this is a thoughtful way to use insurance in a manner that helps everyone. The donor knows his/her wishes will be completed because the gift is secured.

The church can go ahead with needed projects because the funds are assured.

SELL ENDOWMENT POLICIES AT COST

"Bargain Sale" gifts are explained elsewhere, but the same principles work here. The donor has an endowment type policy which has substantially larger cash values than its cost. The donor may not be willing or able to give the entire amount to the church or may wish to tax shelter the appreciated gain. Selling the policy makes good sense in such a situation.

The church purchases the endowment policy for the actual cost of the policy to the donor (the sum of premiums paid). The donor may deduct as a gift the difference between the cost and present value. The difference must also be declared as income but will be washed out with the deduction.

LOAN THE CASH VALUES

In this day of sky-high loan interest rates, many persons have discovered the hidden treasure of low rates for loans from insurance cash values. Why not make these "cheap" loan funds available to the church. Instead of 12 or 13% bank interest for construction or additions, these lines of credit often offer the church interest as low as 6%. Here is a wonderful asset that can be tapped by middle-aged donors cash-poor from college expenses or tied-up capital. "Cheap money" is the next best thing to an outright gift.

TITHE THE POLICY

While tithing one's income remains more a goal than a reality for most people, tithing the proceeds of a life insurance policy is a much more realistic option. It is a lot easier to tithe money we can't keep anyway. All it takes is an amendment to an existing policy. When the church is named for a tithe of the benefits irrevocably (or in a term policy), 10% of the premiums become tax deductible as well.

GET IN LINE

Most insurance policies provide for naming more than one beneficiary. The church ought to be in the succession of beneficiaries *someplace*. Ask to be named co-beneficiary, second beneficiary, remainder beneficiary, or residual beneficiary. Here's how the line-up looks.

1. *Beneficiary*—the person or institution named to receive the policy face values upon death of the insured.

2. *Co-Beneficiary*—a shared form of benefit with death benefits, distributed equally or in some designated proportion among beneficiaries.

3. *Secondary Beneficiary*—the person or institution which receives the proceeds of the policy if the primary beneficiary has already died (or dies simultaneously).

4. *Remainder Beneficiary*—the person or institution which receives the proceeds when both primary and secondary beneficiaries have died.

5. *Residual Beneficiary*—the church receives the remaining benefits of an annuitized policy with guaranteed benefits or cash values.

FOUR TYPES OF "OBSOLETE" LIFE INSURANCE POLICIES

• *Burial Expenses*—Years ago almost everyone made certain they had a $1,000 policy "to bury me with." These policies have long since ceased to be needed (or sufficient!) for that purpose. Why not ask your members to clean out their desk drawers and donate these now unnecessary policies?

• *For support of a spouse no longer living*— Many elderly men are over-insured. Policies they purchased years before to provide for their spouse become unnecessary when the spouse pre-deceases them. Many of these persons would get much satisfaction by giving the policy to the church. Perhaps this would be a good asset with which to fund a memorial gift or endowment.

• *Education Insurance*—A common type of obsolete policy is the one purchased to provide college money in case of death. Often the children are well out of college and financially independent while the policy remains in force. Perhaps these funds would start a good scholarship fund for seminary students or college students from your church.

• *Estate Tax Insurance*—Many are the small businesspersons or farmers who were sold a large insurance policy to pay estate or inheritance taxes. With the provisions of the Economic Recovery Tax Act of 1981, fewer than 5% of families will have any federal estate tax liability. Why not point out this good news to your members with the suggestion that these no longer needed policies be given to the church?

DIVIDEND ASSIGNMENT

Many of your members own "participating" insurance policies. These typically include an annual dividend of rebate of a portion of the premium. Unlike stock dividends which are a form of income, life insurance dividends are considered rebates or returned principal. Therefore these "dividends" are not considered taxable income.

When the dividend is given to the church, however, the gift is fully tax deductible. The net effect is to reduce the income subject to tax from all sources. Here is a simple method in which the deductible gift is the equivalent of a gift twice as large to the donor.

The other nice feature of dividend assignment is that the money given is "painless." Few persons anticipate the dividend check and fewer still use it creatively. By assigning the payment to the church, the money which might otherwise be frivolously spent becomes a tool of ministry and a source of real satisfaction.

13. ASSET REPLENISHMENT

This is not really a use of life insurance as a gift instrument but uses insurance to encourage gift annuities. Here's how it might work.

A donor wishes to establish a $100,000 gift annuity but fears this will unacceptably reduce the estate left for the two children. Asset replenishment allows the purchase of life insurance with the gift annuity income. This income is gifted to the children for use in purchasing whole life insurance placed in an irrevocable insurance trust payable to the children. Note: This trust must contain *Crummey* powers which only a competent attorney can create. Crummey powers provide the equivocal right to make withdrawals necessary to assure the gift tax exclusion.

The key points of Asset Replenishment are:

1. Purchase of a gift annuity from a qualified charity.
2. An immediate tax deduction of the charitable remainder value (depends upon age of donor and type of annuity but is usually about one-third the gift amount).
3. The annuity income is ⅔ tax free.
4. The after-tax annuity income funds the insurance trust for purchase of the life insurance on the donor's life.
5. When the donor dies, the church or charity receives all the gift amount not repaid to the donor (today this may be *more* than the original gift amount).
6. When the donor dies, the children receive the face value of the insurance policy. Note: This is not taxable income to the heirs and will not be counted as part of the probatable estate.
7. The donor has the satisfaction of making a major gift while providing for heirs.

For more information on this intriguing concept, you may wish to contact The Brennan Companies, 1207 Third Ave, P.O. Box 214, Spring Lake, NJ 07762.

14. MEMORIAL GIVING

Memorial gifts offer a unique opportunity to tap two giving motives: 1) interest in the beneficiary project and 2) desire to honor another person. In most memorial gifts both motives are present, but the proportion often varies widely. The church must guard against assumptions about which motive is operative and allow for either to direct the gift.

A good memorial gift emphasis will stress both the church's need to fund various projects with memorials and also the donor's need to express love for the one to be remembered by the gift. This suggests that something more than an appeal to give "to the memorial fund" is necessary. The "fund" concept conjures up images of small gifts piling up toward some unknown project or purchase. Few persons are highly motivated to give to an unknown fund. A better way is to offer several memorial giving options throughout the year—not only upon the occasion of death.

Consider these ongoing giving possibilities:

1. *Altar flowers*—An outstanding vehicle for loved ones to be remembered in a practical and meaningful manner. Schedule sponsors for each Sunday of the year, with a weekly note in the bulletin announcing the donor and the loved one to be memorialized.

2. *Bulletins*—Many persons would be glad to sponsor a week's bulletin costs for an opportunity to name a loved one.

3. *Mission Mother's Day*—Why not give people a chance to honor a living mother or remember a deceased mother with a gift for a special mission project on Mother's Day? One church used this approach with a bulletin insert listing those honored along with the donor and raised the largest single mission offering of the year. Perhaps your women's society could help with these.

4. *Memorial Music*—What better way to honor a faithful choir member than to endow a music fund? Memorial gifts could provide:

a. purchase of music for a week or more

b. sponsorship of a week's share of the music budget (organist salary, choir director, etc.)

c. funds for a special concert, cantata, musical, etc.

d. new robes/stoles for the choir

e. funds for soloists and other special music

5. *Children's Ministries*—Older folks often have a warm spot for anything related to children's ministries. This also gives a wonderful image of a living memorial as one generation remembers a previous generation with gifts serving a succeeding generation. Church school literature, arts and crafts supplies, playground equipment, anything for kids makes a good memorial project.

Here are the Do's and Don'ts of a successful Memorial Gift Program.

DO

- Have an ongoing list of projects and purchases for which memorial gifts would be appropriate and appreciated.
- Include in your list small, medium, and major gift opportunities.
- Notify the family every time a memorial gift is received. Tell who gave the gift, not the amount.
- Contact widows/widowers and surviving children at least annually with a current memorial opportunity.
- Stress "Living Memorials" or endowed projects rather than one-shot purchases. This is a compliment to the deceased for the loved ones to memorialize them in an ongoing manner.
- Give recognition every time a memorial is received. Perhaps a regular newsletter column would stimulate regular memorial gifts.
- Have plenty of Memorial Fund envelopes handy. They should be in each pew and in the narthex and wherever people congregate. In addition, every local funeral home ought to have a good supply.
- Have a Memorial Service at least annually. Some churches do it on All Saints' Day, others soon after the first of the year. Pick whatever works for you. Recognize each member who has died in the past year. Note each memorial gift received. Invite new memorials. One church promoted the day with special invitations to all the immediate family of deceased members and recorded one of the largest attendances and offerings of the year. In addition, new memorials were received every time.

DON'T

- Try to spend every memorial gift or individual's memorial on a separate item. This only fills the church with needless baubles.
- Forget to thank the donors. For many, this will be their first contact with the church.
- Think only in terms of "something for the sanctuary." Unless the item represents a real need, the purchase trivializes the memorial.

15. CHARITABLE GIVING AND TAXES: TEN STRATEGIES

While much has been said and written about the tax consequences of various giving opportunities, *I do not believe that most donors are much impressed by the deductibility of charitable gifts.* The primary motive of donors has always been and, irrespective of tax codes, will continue to be the desire to help.

Nevertheless, a thoughtful stewardship program will include information about taxes, not as a motivator, but as a help for those who are already motivated to give. Wise use of our tax law will enable your donors to give more *at less cost.*

Here are ten giving strategies which may prove helpful to your constituents. As with anything related to the law, it is wise to monitor changes which may alter a particular strategy. Consult an accountant or attorney for advice about the tax consequences of major gifts.

1. Give *appreciated securities.* You will avoid capital gains tax and may deduct the fair market value, even though your cost was much less.

2. *"Give and take."* Instead of giving through your will (which results in no tax advantage to you), give by gift annuity, which allows you to make a gift and take back the income produced by it. This strategy results in an immediate charitable gift deduction for the "remainder value" and a combination of taxable and tax-exempt income for life.

3. Give *appreciated real estate.* As with securities, you avoid tax on capital gains.

4. Give *memorials* instead of flowers. While flowers given in memory of a loved one are not deductible, gifts to a church memorial fund are deductible.

5. Give through *life estate contracts.* You may give your home or family farm while retaining possession of it for life. You receive an immediate deduction, even though the ownership of the property doesn't transfer until your death.

6. Give *life insurance* and deduct the premiums. Another alternative

to the non-deductible bequest is the purchase of life insurance with face value equal to the desired bequest. As long as the church is the owner and beneficiary of the policy, all your premium payments are deductible.

7. Give a *trust*. Unneeded funds could become a trust, the income from which would fund your church pledge forever. You get an immediate deduction of the full trust amount. You can even stretch the deduction over five years.

8. Give by *"Bargain Sale."* Appreciated property which is sold to the charity at less than market value results in a charitable gift of the difference between sale price and market value. Take a deduction of this difference.

9. Give *a year ahead.* Because of the recent increase in the allowable standard deduction, many taxpayers are unable to profit from itemizing deductions. Currently the amounts are $5,000 for married, jointly or surviving spouse, $4,400 for unmarried head of household, and $2,500 for married separate returns, and $3,000 for singles.

   However, careful planning may enable above-the-line deductions. You may, for example, prepay your pledge for a calendar year in December of the previous year. In effect, this prepayment results in two years' worth of giving in the year in which the gift is made. This may enable the donor to exceed the standard deduction amount and itemize. The next year (the year for which the pledge has been prepaid) the donor elects the standard deduction amount. This strategy results in use of itemizing every other year with election of zero bracket in the intervening years.

10. Give with your *interest deduction.* It is a strange quirk of our tax codes that gives individuals a deduction for interest paid on loans while churches, which are tax-exempt, enjoy no such deduction. This suggests that, rather than having the church borrow, individual donors could borrow the funds and give them to the church. The same interest will be paid but at less cost because of the resultant deduction.

Note: Loans other than mortgages or "home equity" loans have only partially deductible interest until 1991, when none of the interest will be deductible.

16. BOTH POCKETS

While I suppose I've *known* it for years, I must attribute to Lyle Schaller the *understanding* that people have two pockets. The first pocket, which might contain loose change, represents current income. This pocket is the resource most churches use exclusively when asking their people for money. Studies show that, no matter what the need, persons giving from the current income pocket will nearly always give a portion of the last two weeks' income. The self-limiting nature of this fund source should be apparent. You will never get more than the last two weeks' pay and usually will get only a fraction of that.

But people have *two* pockets. The second pocket contains, not change, but bills. This pocket represents accumulated resources. While current income has increased steadily over the years, accumulated resources have grown even more dramatically. It is not unusual today for the accumulated resources pocket to contain *100 times* the current income pocket! For retirees the disparity is frequently even greater. Yet churches continue to ask for money from the current pocket.

We do our people a real service when we remind them that: 1) they have two pockets, 2) they may give from either pocket, and 3) they may give more at less cost if they know from which pocket to give.

Planned giving helps people discover ways to put both pockets to work.

17. LIFE INCOME GIFTS

One of the fastest growing areas of charitable giving is giving through life income plans. In each of these strategies, the donor makes a charitable gift while retaining income from the gift assets for the donor's life. This becomes a way in which persons who had planned to make a charitable bequest through their wills may achieve the same end while enjoying two significant benefits: first, the donor receives income without the need to make investment or money management decisions; in addition, the donor receives important income tax advantages.

A gift annuity is a legal contract between the charity and the donor. The charity is obligated to provide a stated amount to the donor for life (or for the lives of two persons such as a married couple). The amount of the gift annuity is determined by the gift amount and the donor's age. Rates are established every three years by the Committee on Gift Annuities. Following is a chart showing the current single-life annuity rates.

In addition to the income of the gift annuity, the donor receives two income tax advantages—first, a charitable gift deduction equal to the present value of the future remainder interest (often ⅓ to ½ of the amount put into the annuity). Also, the income of the annuity will be partly tax-free. The tax-free nature of this income (typically ⅓ to ⅔ of the annuity) is due to the fact that it is considered return of principal.

Life income trusts have many of the characteristics of gift annuities but additional flexibility. Unlike the case with a gift annuity, the donor may choose the desired rate of trust income. The lower the rate of income established, the higher the charitable deduction (and vice versa). In general, trust income will be taxable. However, the donor may choose a charitable remainder *annuity* trust (in which the income will never vary) or a charitable remainder *unitrust* in which the income is based on a percentage of the trust assets. In a unitrust, well-managed funds often enable the donor to enjoy income that increases each year. This is a significant feature for those concerned with inflation.

Selecting a gift annuity or life income trust is a "judgment call." Among the factors to be considered are:

1) Costs of establishing and administering the gift. Gift annuities

frequently are less expensive to administer and usually are more effective for gifts of $25,000 or less.

2) Source of funding. Appreciated property is usually best for funding trust while gift annuities work best when funded with cash.

3) Age of the donor(s). Because annuities are significantly related to donor age while only the tax deduction of trusts is age-related, older donors may find gift annuities preferable.

When persons notify you that they have included the church in their will, you may wish to do more than thank them. Show them how their future gift might bring current advantages through life income gift plans.

Uniform gift annuity rates—To determine the size of payments which one person will receive for gift annuity, multiply the rate shown below for the person's age by the value of the property used to create the annuity.

Single Life

Age	Rate	Age	Rate	Age	Rate
50	6.5%	64	7.2%	78	9.1%
51	6.6	65	7.3	79	9.4
52	6.6	66	7.4	80	9.6
53	6.6	67	7.5	81	9.9
54	6.7	68	7.6	82	10.1
55	6.7	69	7.7	83	10.4
56	6.8	70	7.8	84	10.6
57	6.8	71	7.9	85	10.9
58	6.9	72	8.0	86	11.1
59	6.9	73	8.2	87	11.4
60	7.0	74	8.3	88	11.6
61	7.0	75	8.5	89	11.8
62	7.1	76	8.7	90-over	12.0
63	7.1	77	8.9		

APPENDICES

Appendix A

HOW TO PROCEED WITH YOUR WILLS EMPHASIS PREPARATION

A. Make a Plan

1. For receiving and administering gifts
2. For sharing the plan with the congregation
3. For how to manage funds
4. For developing a statement of purpose for the funds
5. For promoting and interpreting the program regularly

B. Management with Integrity

1. Develop wise investment between income and growth.
2. Use income in harmony with agreements and bequests.
3. For your own protection consider using your denomination's foundation(s).
4. Avoid conflicts of interest.
5. Do not borrow against principal.
6. Give complete financial report to congregation annually.
7. Distribute income at least annually.

C. Make Suggestions on How to Give

1. Unrestricted
2. Designated
3. Contingency
4. Memorials
5. Trusts and annuities
6. Life insurance
7. Various kinds of property
8. Percentage of estate
9. Residue of estate
10. Other kinds of gifts

D. Acceptance and Investment

1. The gift must be in harmony with the church's practices and standards.
2. It must be in harmony with the social principles of your denomination.

WILLS, MEMORIALS, AND ESTATE PLANNING COMMITTEE

Many churches already have a functioning Memorials Committee which keeps records and makes occasional recommendations for use of memorials moneys.

I suggest that you work through your church's Committee on Nomination and Personnel and ask for a committee to pick up all three of these emphases, so that they will not need to compete with each other. The committee can be called the "Wills, Memorials, and Estate Planning Committee."

Members of this committee should equip themselves for a year-round emphasis within their church.

SUGGESTED MEMBERSHIP OF THE COMMITTEE

1. Pastor
2. A highly regarded middle-aged to older woman
3. A young couple
4. A person with stewardship interest
5. A lawyer or trust officer or C.P.A.
6. A representative from the Trustees
7. A person with mission outreach interest
8. A former Memorials Committee member or members
9. Other

Persons recruited for membership on the Wills, Memorials, and Estate Planning Committee should make, or update, their wills prior to service.

ADMINISTRATIVE BOARD DETERMINES POLICIES AND/OR GUIDELINES

1. The bequest or trust is referred to the Trustees.

2. The Trustees report to the Charge Conference.

3. The pastor writes a letter of thanks to the family.

4. The Trustees write a letter of acceptance to the lawyer.

5. The church follows the designation or the restrictions of bequest.

6. If the gift is undesignated, the Administrative Board should determine in advance its percentage of distribution, such as: 40% for program, including scholarships, etc.; 40% for building, upkeep, or expansion; 20% for mission outreach outside the local church and local community.

   or

   50% for local church upkeep, expansion, program, and community outreach; and 50% for state and world outreach.

7. Committee on Finance is responsible for disbursement of funds.

8. Wills, Memorials, and Estate Planning Committee is responsible for year-round emphasis of will, memorials, and annuities.

9. Possible use of your conference foundation for investment care and for annuities.

Administration of your planned giving program using this pattern of management will eliminate the need to create a cumbersome layer of new administrative entities such as local church foundations. In each case, keep it simple. Use your conference's planned giving offices for advice and administrative assistance.

Appendix B
SAMPLE LIFE ESTATE
AGREEMENT

NOTE: This legal instrument is a SAMPLE only. State laws vary widely; therefore, you should first consult your own legal counsel. The use of generalized documents for specific applications is not recommended.

This AGREEMENT made and entered into by and between *(name)*, of *(city and state)*, hereinafter referred to as Grantor, and *(institution)*, a nonprofit charitable corporation of the State of_____ hereinafter referred to as
_____.

WITNESSETH;

WHEREAS Grantor has executed and delivered to *(institution)* a Warranty Deed conveying to *(institution)* the following described real estate, to wit:

(Include Property description here)

in which deed Grantor has reserved unto himself/herself a life estate; IT IS THEREFORE AGREED by and between the parties hereto:

1) That Grantor during the full term of his/her natural life shall be entitled to the right of possession and occupancy in and to the above described real estate and the rents, income, and profits arising therefrom.
2) That Grantor shall pay the real estate taxes levied and assessed against said real estate during his/her lifetime.
3) That *(institution)* will not sell or convey its remainder interest in said real estate during the lifetime of Grantor.
4) In accepting the deed which conveys the title to *(institution)* subject to the life estate, *(institution)* agrees that if Grantor is required to use the full title to this property *(institution)* will join with him/her in the execution of whatever documents may be required to assure him/her of the full use thereof.
5) It is mutually understood and agreed by the parties to this agreement that the sole purpose of this grant is that the proceeds from the sale of the property shall be paid to *(institution)*, to be used in carrying out its corporate objectives and purposes.

IN WITNESS WHEREOF the parties have executed this agreement this day of
_____, 19____.

Grantor

(Name of Institution)

By

Appendix C
ESTABLISHING A LOCAL CHURCH ENDOWMENT FUND

SECTION I. ACCEPTANCE OF THE GIFT

A. Appropriate 1988 *Discipline* paragraphs.

1. A Charge Conference shall be held "to direct the Board of Trustees with respect to the acceptance or rejection of any and all conveyances, grants, gifts, donations, legacies, bequests, or devices, absolute or in trust, for the use and benefit of the local church, and to require the administration of any such trust in accordance with the terms and provisions." (¶ 2528.3)

2. "Subject to the direction of the Charge Conference . . . the Board of Trustees shall receive and administer all bequests made to the local church; shall receive and administer all trusts; shall invest all trust funds of the local church in conformity with the law."(¶ 2532.4).

B. Arrangements for the calling of a Charge Conference are made in the usual procedure: the request of such a Charge or Church Conference to be called by the district superintendent for the specific purpose if occurring at a time other than the annual Charge Conference, generally in the fall of each year.

C. After appropriate notification is received of the intent of the gift, generally through the administrator or personal representative of the estate, a committee may be called together to review the stipulations and restrictions of such a gift, if any, outright or in trust, and whether the benefit of the gift will indeed benefit the ministry and congregation of Anywhere UMC. After appropriate study, generally by persons on the Trustees, the significant program area to be affected, and representative(s) of the Council on Ministries, a recommendation shall be brought to the Charge Conference on the acceptance or rejection of the gift.

D. Action of the Charge Conference is a crucial legal requirement that provides for the proper acceptance within the structure of the church of the legal commitment encumbered when one accepts a gift in trust or through an estate gift given under will.

E. The *Discipline* then directs under ¶2532 that the administration of the bequest or trust shall be managed by the Trustees of the church. They are the legal incorporated body of each local church. Anywhere UMC may further direct Trustees to have set up or organized Endowment Fund Trustees or a local church foundation so that separate actions and talents may be present in dealing with certain kinds of financial matters relating to estates and trusts. The format of a local church endowment fund or foundation trustees shall be established by a vote at a Charge or Church Conference called expressly for that purpose.

F. Each congregation should establish the *criteria* under which gifts of any size or amount, any kind of property, whether real estate, stock or bond or cash, will be considered and favorably received. Such questions as: immediate sale or postponed sale of stock, immediate sale or first offer on property, investment in government securities, US savings certificates or bonds, money market accounts with brokerage houses, deposit with or co-mingling of funds with other long-term investment assets of the local church or assignment to the United Methodist Foundation of the Annual Conference for separate investment care.

For what purposes will gifts be received? Only in one area as in mission education or physical plant maintenance and development or a combination? Will the church receive and handle gifts for the benefit of other United Methodist institutions such as United Methodist retirement homes or Children's Village? Or will those gifts be immediately turned over to those other related institutions? Will the church receive and manage funds a portion of which shall be used for non-United Methodist charities such as a secular college or university, hospital, or youth organizations?

SECTION II. THE MANAGEMENT OF THE FUND

Prior to receiving gifts, preferably, a format for the management of principal and distribution of income will have been decided.

A. Who will manage the funds? Will these be the Trustees of the local church, a combination of Trustees and other skilled parties within the church? An investment committee that is accountable and responsible to the Trustees of the local church? Will the Trustees, through the election process, have the skill for the management of such funds? Will the church hire or appoint a separate institution, such as a Trust Company, a brokerage house of the United Methodist Foundation to manage the funds for it? What is the price you are willing to pay and how is this price to be determined?

B. Under what criteria will the funds be invested? The Social Principles of the church (¶¶70-76) and in accordance with the protocols of the General Council on Finance and Administration of The United Methodist Church. Copies are available from the United Methodist Conference Center.

SECTION III. DISTRIBUTION OF INCOME

A. The church must decide who will determine where the income goes.

B. Numerous considerations should be carefully detailed.

1. Obviously, income from a designated gift must be spent only in the designated area. Example: A gift to generate income for camping scholarships can only go for camping scholarships, but that may be narrowly or broadly interpreted. A narrow interpretation might be only for summer camps sponsored on a week-long basis by the Annual Conference. A broader definition might include weekend youth retreats, work camps or projects on mission sites in the state or around the world, adult travel seminars or other similar off-site educational church-sponsored experiences. The body which decides how the gift limitation shall be implemented must be identified clearly within the structure of the local United Methodist church.

2. Gifts—principal restricted to be invested—unrestricted income.

3. Totally unrestricted income or principal.

C. We strongly recommend that the investing body (Trustees, etc.) not be the body that determines how the income is to be expended. That, in our opinion, should be decided by the regular budgeting process within the local church, generally the Council on Ministries, in consultation with the Finance Committee and ratification by the Administrative Board.

D. The investing body should, however, forecast as carefully and precisely as possible the amount of income to be available for distribution in the designated and undesignated categories so that the annual budget-building process can proceed in an orderly manner.

E. Income from such invested funds should be used for enrichment programs or augmenting and adding to the basic program and structure of the local church. these funds should rarely, if ever (NEVER?), be used for the basic operating budget of the church: namely, utilities, pastoral support, Conference apportionments. However, additional program, innovative ministries that need seed money, additional staff to the basic staff of the church, special mission support or pilot project funds within your local church or community, statewide or general church mission project for Advance Specials, major facility improvement, major capital repair or addition may also receive benefits from these kinds of invested funds.

F. Principal should rarely, if ever (NEVER?), be withdrawn. Extreme and overwhelming circumstances must be present for such drastic action to occur. Nearly unanimous action should be required in the bylaws of the fund in order to withdraw principal from the endowment or foundation funds in a local church. An example of such a restriction might be 15% of the congregational membership attending a Church Conference and 90% voting in favor of such a withdrawal. The broadest range of support should be received for this kind of drastic action.

G. As above, the amendment procedure for amending the bylaws of the endowment fund or foundation should be as restrictive or as nearly restrictive. The problem: As you will note in the above item F, if the bylaw amendment procedure is two-thirds of those voting at a Charge Conference, a regular Charge Conference could amend the withdrawal procedure. Therefore, the restrictions on removing funds from the endowment or the foundation could be decided by a much less representative or participatory body.

Appendix D
GUIDELINES FOR ANYWHERE
UNITED METHODIST CHURCH
ENDOWMENT FUND

THE PURPOSE

The ANYWHERE UMC Endowment Fund of ANYWHERE United Methodist Church, ANYWHERE, USA is established for the purpose of providing members and friends the opportunity to make charitable gifts to Anywhere UMC that will become a permanent endowment of financial support and a living memorial to those whom the church has served.

ADMINISTRATION

The Anywhere UMC Endowment Fund will be administered by the Endowment Fund Committee as assigned by the Board of Trustees. The membership of the Committee shall consist of nine members plus two ex-officio members as follows:

Finance Chairperson of the Board of Trustees
Treasurer of the Church
Chairperson of the Finance Committee
The Pastor (ex-officio)
The Lay Leader (ex-officio)
Six members-at-large elected by the Administrative Board

The six members-at-large shall be nominated by the Nominating Committee of the church and elected for three-year terms by the Administrative Board. Initially, the members shall be phased in on two-, four-, and six-year terms, so that each succeeding year a new member will be elected for a full three-year term.

Each year at its first meeting, the Endowment Fund Committee shall elect three officers: President, Secretary, and Treasurer.

The following are the responsibility of the Endowment Fund Committee:

1. Encourage endowment gifts for the Endowment Fund.

2. Be responsible for the investment and management of the Endowment Fund.
3. Present at least one program annually to inform the congregation of the opportunities through the Endowment Fund.
4. Prepare bulletin/newsletter announcements and appropriate brochures for distribution.

The Endowment Fund Committee shall prepare and present a report at least annually to the Charge Conference, the Board of Trustees, and the Administrative Board.

INVESTMENT OF ENDOWMENT FUND

The Anywhere UMC Endowment Fund is designed to offer a portfolio balanced through a diversified group of quality securities. The Fund's three-fold investment objectives are:

1. Conservation of principal for the effective maintenance of purchasing power
2. Regular income at a reasonable rate
3. Growth of income and principal over and above that necessary to offset rises in the cost-of-living

All gifts received for the Anywhere UMC Endowment Fund shall be invested, and only the income from the investments shall be transferred for disbursement. The income from the investment of the Anywhere UMC Endowment Fund will be managed by the Endowment Fund Committee and may be transferred to the Finance Committee of the Administrative Board of the church to support the financial needs of Anywhere Church. *(Discipline, ¶2427)*

WAYS TO GIVE

The primary emphasis of Anywhere UMC Endowment Fund is to encourage members and friends to consider a once-in-a-lifetime gift above their current contributions. Most often such a gift will be part of a person's estate plan. Some methods of giving are:

Bequest—Bequest through a will is the most frequent form of an endowment gift, largely because it can be a means of making a substantial gift to the church without diminishing the assets available to the donor during his or her lifetime. Important estate tax savings can result from this type of contribution, since bequests to Anywhere United Methodist Church may be deducted completely from the total estate in determining estate taxes.

The drafting of one's will is, of course, a job for one's attorney. Counsel from the pastor or Endowment Fund Committee will be available upon request in assisting persons in drafting an appropriate bequest and the terms and conditions for each gift.

Testamentary Trust—A substantial bequest can be made to Anywhere United Methodist Church while at the same time providing income for the donor's family or others during their lifetimes. The Testamentary Trust can be a way of making such a bequest.

Life Income Trust—For those individuals who wish to give substantially toward the strength of the church and yet wish to be assured of financial security, the life income program offers great opportunity.

Gifts of Life Insurance—Life insurance, properly handled, offers one of the most attractive ways of benefiting the Anywhere UMC Endowment Fund substantially at a relatively low cost to the donor.

Gifts of Real Estate—The Endowment Fund Committee will be pleased to talk with any member or friend who desires the possibility of donating real estate for support of the Anywhere UMC Endowment Fund.

Gifts of Securities—Securities that have appreciated greatly in value and have been held for more than six months may be advantageously given to the Anywhere UMC Endowment Fund. There are various tax advantages for doing so, and the Endowment Committee will be pleased to outline them.

Gifts of Cash—Although the Anywhere UMC Endowment Fund was not primarily established for gifts of cash, it is a popular way of contributing to the Endowment Fund.

GIFTS IN HONOR, GIFTS IN MEMORY

Gifts to the Anywhere UMC Endowment Fund may be anonymous or given in honor of a living person(s) or in memory of a deceased one.

All gifts are recorded in the Anywhere UMC Endowment Book of Remembrance.

FOUNDERS

To encourage the growth of the Anywhere UMC Endowment Fund, members and friends designating a substantial contribution to the Endowment Fund in the first year will be named Founders and be appropriately recognized.

DISSOLUTION

The Anywhere UMC endowment Fund will be dissolved only in the event of the complete dissolution of Anywhere United Methodist Church, at which time these assets shall become the property of the Annual Conference of The United Methodist Church.

ILLUSTRATIONS

1. By permission of Kregel Publications, Charles Cartwright.
2. By permission of Baker Books, *Instant Cartoons for Church Newsletters,* compiled by George W. Knight.
3. Ibid.
4. By permission of Johnny Hart and NAS, Inc.
5. By permission of Kregel Publications, Charles Cartwright.
6. Ibid.
7. By permission of Wayne C. Barrett.
8. By permission of Kregel Publications, Charles Cartwright.
9. Ibid.
10. By permission of Baker Books, *Instant Cartoons for Church Newsletters,* compiled by George W. Knight.
11. By permission of Johnny Hart and NAS, Inc.
12. By permission of Kregel Publications, Charles Cartwright.
13. By permission of Wayne C. Barrett.
14. By permission of Johnny Hart and NAS, Inc.
15. By permission of Baker Books, *Instant Cartoons for Church Newsletters,* compiled by George W. Knight.